Going Forward Looking Back

Reflections on two decades of Irish charity work
in Central and Eastern Europe

```
This book belongs to
Geraldine O'Sullivan
and to her friends.
```

Going Forward Looking Back

Reflections on two decades of Irish charity work
in Central and Eastern Europe

Published by
Eastern Europe Aid & Development Network

Published in February 2011 by
Eastern Europe Aid & Development Network
c/o Ashfield House
Derry Road
Durrow
Co. Laois
Ireland

Copyright © 2011 Eastern Europe Aid & Development Network
Edited by Frances Haworth

All rights reserved. No part of this publication may be reproduced in any form
or by any means – graphic, electronic or mechanical, including photocopying, recording,
taping or information storage and retrieval systems – without the prior written
permission of the copyright owners. Applications for permission to use
extracts should be addressed to the publisher.

Opinions expressed in the interviews in this publication are those of
the individual interviewees and do not necessarily reflect the opinions of
the Editorial Committee or of Eastern Europe Aid & Development Network.

www.easterneurope.ie

ISBN: 978-0-9567856-0-2

Published by Eastern Europe Aid & Development Network, 2011

Printed by Colour Books, Dublin.
Design: Anú Design, Tara

Contents

About the Network ... vii
Acknowledgements ... viii
Introduction ... ix

'Go in and talk to people and involve them' ... 1
Liam Grant (Belarus, Romania)

'Work in partnership and in pace with people' ... 5
Caroline McGreal (Romania)

'Find people who will work with you' ... 11
Herbert Armitage & Noel Deane (Belarus)

'To change things you have to stay in the equation' ... 17
Conor Hughes (Romania)

'There has to be give and take' ... 23
Ned Hayden & Brian O'Sullivan (Belarus)

'Focus on what you're good at' ... 31
Stuart Wilson (Belarus, Georgia)

'Everyone has a different skill' ... 37
Jim McQuaid (Romania)

'Create self-sufficiency' ... 43
Stephen Conway (Georgia, Romania, Belarus)

'Be open to cooperation' ... 49
Simon & Deena Walsh (Belarus)

'Treat everyone as an individual' ... 55
Audrey Cranston (Romania)

'Do more with the money'   61
Henry Deane (Belarus)

'Persuade the decision makers'   67
John Mulligan (Romania)

'It's all about trust'   73
Stephen Wilson (Albania)

'Put money into the economy'   79
Michael Kinsella (Moldova)

'Have an investor mentality'   85
Patricia Keane (Bosnia & Herzegovina)

'Educate across the board'   93
Mairie Cregan (Romania)

'Do your research'   99
Tom McEnaney (Belarus)

'Deal with the right people'   107
Fiona Corcoran (Ukraine, Kazakhstan)

'The direct approach is best'   113
Tajma Kapic & Svenn Braamark (Bosnia & Herzegovina, Kosovo, Albania)

'Long term improvements need a long term plan'   119
Michael Gannon & Moya McCann (Albania)

'Change the hearts and minds of the administration'   125
Debbie Deegan (Russia)

'Think objectively'   131
Joe McGrath (Belarus)

'Stop before you intervene'   137
Fiona Dowling (Romania)

'Keep things small so you can handle them'   145
Kieran Byrne, Pat Whelan, Fr Celsus Tierney (Romania, Albania)

List of Interviewees   151
Resource Directory   153

About the Network

In 2009, the Eastern Europe Aid & Development Network (EEADN) was created by and for Irish charities and voluntary groups working in Eastern Europe to facilitate improved effectiveness through communication and cooperation. Find out more about the work of the Network and sign up for membership at www.easterneurope.ie.

About this Publication

The text is based on a series of interviews carried out by Frances Haworth & Dr Patty Gray between August and December 2010. The interviews were recorded, transcribed and edited for inclusion in the publication. In so far as possible, this resource seeks to comply with the National Disability Authority's guidelines on producing accessible publications and the Dóchas Code of Conduct on Images and Messages.

Editorial Committee

Frances Haworth (Editor) – Frances coordinates the EEAD Network activities, as part of her role with Comber – for a future without orphanages. She also helped establish Moldova Vision in 2006, a voluntary group supporting Moldovan migrants in Ireland and social projects at home.

Dr Patty Gray – Patty lectures in Anthropology at NUI Maynooth and has carried out field research in Russia. Her areas of interest include the impact of overseas aid on Russian, Eastern European and (formerly) socialist societies.

John Mulligan – John has worked in Romania since 1991 and set up Focus on Romania in the late 1990s. He is the author of three books including *Dancing on the Waves* – an account of his experiences in Romania's orphanages.

Helen Walmsley – Helen coordinates the International Volunteer Projects Programme at Voluntary Service International. She previously worked with 'Fundatia Pentru o Viata mai Buna' (through Health Action Overseas) in Romania.

Acknowledgements

Sincere thanks to all those who helped develop this publication, most especially those who took part in interviews and shared their stories. Due to space restrictions, not all of the interviews have been included in the printed publication – the full range is available online at www.easterneurope.ie.

Nuala Crowe-Taft deserves special mention for her role as facilitator of the workshop series which led to this publication. Thanks are due to Áine Costigan, Selam Desta and Catherine Behan from Dtalk and Hans Zomer and Holy Ramanankasina from Dóchas for their encouragement and advice. Particular thanks also to Aisling O'Kane and Oana Alexan, who have interned with the Network over the past year. Aisling also compiled the resources section of this publication.

The interviews were transcribed by a team of dedicated individuals from around the world through United Nations Online Volunteering. Thanks to Alicia Dorr, Jessica Anne Wise, Sarah Shirley, Tara Green, Eleanor Wragg, Marta Jankovic, Kari Kitiuk, Mary McKeown, Matty McGray, Olivia Cook, Coralie Young, Matilde Mbulo and Jennifer McDonald.

Thanks also to those who submitted photographs for inclusion; these have been referenced individually where used and a further selection is also available on the Network website.

Eastern Europe Aid & Development Network gratefully acknowledge the financial support of Electric Aid, Dtalk, Irish Research Council for Humanities and Social Sciences, and Comber – for a future without orphanages, without which this publication would not have been possible.

Introduction

This publication has come about as a result of a new initiative, the Eastern Europe Aid & Development Network, which was established in 2009. The Network aims to bring together Irish charities working in Central and Eastern Europe to share information, advice and learning with each other.

This resource was developed to capture the stories and reflections of individual volunteers and aid workers based on their personal experiences.

Most Irish charities in Eastern Europe have been in operation since the early 1990s, and two decades later, this seems an appropriate juncture to pause and take stock of what has been achieved, reflect on the lessons learned and consider the future.

Ireland's response to crises in the region over the past twenty years has been generous and heartfelt – we reached across Europe and gave what we could. Millions of euros of funding, hundreds of convoys of aid and thousands of volunteers have left Ireland for Belarus, Romania, Bosnia, Moldova, Georgia, Albania and surrounding countries. It was an instinctive response to disasters unfolding before our eyes – the nuclear accident at Chernobyl, the 'opening' of Romania's orphanages, the Bosnian conflict and the economic collapse after the fall of the Soviet Union. Since the 1990s, there have been considerable economic and social developments in the region and the European Union has enlarged eastwards. Despite this, high levels of inequality and poverty persist. Today there are up to 100 Irish groups, mostly volunteer based, still working in the region.

The past two decades have seen the lives of many in Ireland and the region become inextricably interwoven. Communities all around Ireland have hosted thousands of children from Chernobyl and beyond. Countless Irish volunteers from all walks of life have spent time in little known villages and orphanages from Romania to the far reaches of Russia and Kazakhstan. It is difficult to evaluate this level of involvement and to define the impact on the individuals involved. And yet, between us, we have amassed a huge amount of knowledge and learning that can be shared with others.

The purpose of this publication is to capture that knowledge and to document, not only the fascinating social history of Ireland's aid efforts in the region, but also the lessons learned. There is a real sense of self-reflection in the interviews within this publication which is honest and often moving. Irish volunteers who went to work in Eastern Europe came from quite varied backgrounds, often with little or no experience in overseas aid – it was an emotional response to appalling circumstances. Over the years, understanding of countries and communities has deepened, relationships have developed and for many the commitment to the work has become stronger. Many of us have puzzled over the same problems, made the same mistakes and learned some common lessons.

So what can we learn from each other about being effective in the countries where we work? Although these interviews do not define the story of every Irish volunteer in the region, they capture a good cross section of experiences in different countries, organisations and types of activity. For most, the biggest single lesson learned centres on the importance of communicating and really listening to the people we work with, understanding that an Irish solution is not always best – a simple enough basis on which to operate; but one which can take years to truly understand. When faced with abject need, the desire to act quickly can often override all other considerations. Many of us have learned over time to take a slower, more considered approach.

Some interviewees talk about the importance of training and education, using local resources, avoiding corruption and thinking about the long term sustainability of their work. Others focus on the reform and closure of orphanages and institutions, and evolving practices in working with disability. Some are concerned with political and administrative reform from the top down and others with helping from the ground up, supporting families and children in their homes. Some are starting to think for the first time that their work in the region might be coming to an end; while for others there is still more to be done. It is encouraging for the future of the Network that so many people speak of the importance of charities cooperating instead of competing.

Achieving effectiveness and accountability in the not-for-profit sector is a unique and often challenging responsibility. There is a general assumption in the West that all charities working abroad must be doing useful work – though many individuals with experience in the field would not agree. Too often difficult questions about overseas aid are not asked – Why are we here? What has given us the right to intervene in other people's lives? The interviews pose some difficult questions and put forward some potential answers. Most importantly, this book seeks to emphasize the importance of reflecting on our work, of taking the time to ask questions and engage in dialogue with others. It is hoped that this publication will also inspire and celebrate the achievements of Irish volunteers who have spent decades striving to improve the quality of life of vulnerable and disadvantaged people across the region.

It was a privilege to work on this project and to interview those involved. We hope others can benefit as much from reading the interviews as we have from listening to them. For the purposes of variety the interviews are edited to include a range of topics and themes, not all of which were the main focus of the interview in question. We have endeavoured to do justice to the stories people told us.

Frances Haworth
On behalf of the Editorial Committee

'Go in and talk to people and involve them'

–Liam Grant

Liam (63) is a paramedic from Waterford. He founded **Chernobyl Aid Ireland** in 1998 to work in Grozovo orphanage in Belarus. Chernobyl Aid Ireland has carried out extensive renovation and support work at the orphanage and brings over one hundred children to Ireland each year for rest and recuperation holidays.

> We've learned a lot. In the early days, everything was a rush to get things working and do the best we can. We came in there and wanted to change everything. A couple of years into it, we realised the staff weren't talking to us and asked 'is something wrong here?' So, we sat down and talked to them. We told them what we were about and what we were trying to do.

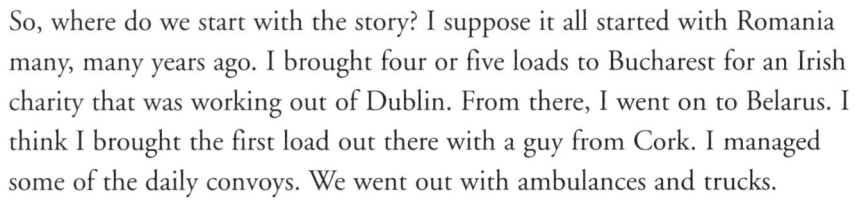

So, where do we start with the story? I suppose it all started with Romania many, many years ago. I brought four or five loads to Bucharest for an Irish charity that was working out of Dublin. From there, I went on to Belarus. I think I brought the first load out there with a guy from Cork. I managed some of the daily convoys. We went out with ambulances and trucks.

Then I decided that we would like to do something just in one specific place. We got a group of guys together and went out and did a survey. We travelled all over Belarus. So, we found this orphanage [Grozovo]. It was an ex-military barracks about 120 miles south of Minsk. There were two hundred kids there

Convoy of aid from Ireland to Belarus, April 2010. *Photo: Chernobyl Orphans Fund*

from the age of seven to eighteen. They were living in squalor. They were living in really bad conditions. No showers. No toilets. There were two or three kids in each of the beds. It was just really bad. We decided that even though we had no money we'd go home and come back out when the weather got better and do something about it. We went back home and got volunteers together. We got the building stuff that we needed for toilets and showers and headed off.

So, we decided to do a five-year plan there. The five years came and went. Every year in May and September, sometimes we had a hundred volunteers working. The place was starting to change. It was really getting a lot better. First of all, we got the living accommodations all sorted out. The accommodation that the kids are living in now is as good as any hotel you could find. Most of the classrooms are all done and brightened up. There are still a few to be done. There is a computer room there … home economics, a library, and a gym. You name it, it's there. Everything has come out of Ireland.

When we started off, the kids were living there with no hope. They had no place to go. Going to college they had no interest in. A lot of them would have ended up in prison as their parents were or on the drink or whatever. Now, the kids are going to decent colleges and universities.

Two years ago, we had a group of kids there that we had from the age of seven. They had been with us all through the years. They couldn't wait to get out. They were really excited. They had done their last bell there and they were all going to colleges and universities. They were really, really happy about getting out. So, I left Belarus and got home. The phone started hopping. The kids were ringing and calling. They wanted to get back. They hadn't realised what they had to face. They had been living with two or three kids their whole life and here they were now living with six strangers. That was traumatic for them. Now, they are coming back and they are talking to the classes that are leaving. They are telling their stories. It's working out very well.

The blocks are like apartments now with a kitchen and sitting room. They can get themselves ready for the outside world. The respect they have for all the equipment there and the pride they have in where they live ... it's really marvellous. The pride their teachers have in them is good.

Some of the kids that are coming to Ireland now are eighteen or nineteen years old. They've been coming to the same families since they were seven. Most of them come to Ireland twice a year – at Christmas and again in the summer time. They see a different way of life. It does inspire them. It has given them something to live for I think.

The president has promised to close all the orphanages in Belarus and put the children in fostering. The number of kids is dropping and a lot of the orphanages are closing. They needed to close anyway, because they were in a really bad state. If the fostering programme works out, it's great. They are leaving a decent orphanage so you would hope that the fostering family is good. From experience and what I've seen ... I've visited kids that are being fostered that I know very well ... some of them are lucky and they are with lovely families. Some of them would have been better off in the orphanage. They are hungry. They would be, honestly, better off in the orphanage. That's only a small percentage though ...

We've got a guarantee from the authorities that Grozovo will be one of the last places to go. It'll go eventually. They are talking about it being called a 'Children's Village' now. Many years ago in Ireland, there were orphanages all over the place. Down the road, they will eventually go I think.

We've learned a lot. In the early days, everything was a rush to get things working and do the best we can. We came in there and wanted to change everything. A couple of years into it, we realised the staff weren't talking to us and we asked, 'Is something wrong here?' So we sat down and talked to them. We told them what we were about and what we were trying to do. We got them to work with us. That end of it is really good now. We get on brilliantly with all of the staff and especially the director. The local authorities are involved as well and people from Minsk. They all come and visit.

Looking back at it, what we had done was totally wrong ... not involving them with the plans and sitting down with them and talking with them about what we were going to do. But we're over that now. It takes time. They were walking past us and giving us dirty looks. We said, 'What the hell are we doing wrong? What the hell is going on? Why aren't you working with us?' But it turns out that we weren't working with them. We hadn't discussed anything with them.

Probably, at times, we thought we were great people: 'We've come here all this distance to do this. We got the work done.' We have a totally different attitude now. Like the one thing that we learned there, just because you're Irish and you have the strength and ability to do it, don't be a bully ... go in and talk to people and involve them as well. It works much better.

Nearly all the Irish charities work together in some way or another. Anytime we would come back from a trip, if there were any new laws or something changed at the border or anything, we'd ring everyone and tell them. All the groups going out will do the same. The same with aid ... if there is a donation of something to a charity that they don't need or don't have any use for, they'll ring around to the other charities and ask if they'll take it.

Belarus is a bit like Ireland in the early years. I remember going to school with Wellington boots or even with no shoes. The poverty where I was brought up was serious. Nobody had any money. That's a bit like what Belarus is like now. Belarus is probably a bit worse. We were happy with the bit we had, which wasn't much. It's great being able to give something back.

I would advise anyone starting out to find some place that really needs help. Find out what the needs are. Find out first of all from the local authorities and the people in Minsk what their plans are for that particular place. It's happened in the past where Irish people have come in to an orphanage for a few years and when they come back the next time, it's closed. You have to do the ground work nowadays especially with so many places closing.

Some people don't believe in staying in the same place and staying there too long. Like I said, we had the five-year plan. Thirteen years later, we're still there. It's not going to change that much in the next few years. As long as I have the strength to keep going and get the support of the Irish people, we'll still be going there anyway. It's going to change year by year. There are always kids in dire straights. It's up and down all the time.

'Work in partnership and in pace with people'

–Caroline McGreal

Caroline (35) is an occupational therapist living in Monaghan. She travelled to Romania to work as a volunteer with **Tanner Romanian Mission** in 2002 for a year and has stayed involved ever since. The Tanners are an American couple who opened residential homes for profoundly disabled children from an orphanage in Nicoresti.

> I think a lot of people went out as trainers and educators who weren't trainers and educators. Who had trained them or educated them to culturally impart information in another language, in another culture, in another place? And I think people took a little bit of liberty, because there was no person saying, 'Stop, I'm not ready for this, I want to take it at this pace.' And in any therapeutic relationship, that's not how I've been trained to work. We work in partnership and in pace with people and you give them as much as they can take on board or as much as they are asking for at the particular time.

From an early age I was interested in Romania and no other country in particular. I think it was the media coverage in the late eighties, early nineties, because I would have been in secondary school. I would have started secondary school in '88, so in those early years I remember the images and I remember the Anneka Rice Challenge and Daniel O'Donnell and things from TV and Christmas appeals and I remember the orphanage pictures.

At that time I realised that there was very little debriefing in Eastern Europe; there was very little emotional support. You were seeing children in a very vulnerable state. There was very little pre-training, there was very little debriefing and so there was very little success. So people came home and new people went out and it was this constant cycle of lots of people and I didn't want to be in that cycle.

I had spoken to people through my church; I was really fortunate that a lot of people had done mission work before and lots of people gave me different details about training and about taking time for yourself and reflection and what I needed to do. I suppose because I was going to a Christian organisation and I was a Christian myself, so I was hugely supported – financially, spiritually, every way. Whereas, I think if people went on their own strength and didn't have that support behind them, that it was very difficult for people and they maybe resented that the Romanians weren't thankful or grateful. Because they had given up something and people didn't even say thank you. A lot of people said that: 'They didn't even say thank you.'

I didn't want to go as a health professional to an orphanage, because a lot of health professionals had gone and done that and I didn't see it, for me, as being successful. The feedback from health professionals would have been that it was a traumatic time… the things they tried to do only worked when they were there. And that would have been a resounding thing from lots of people – their feeling that it didn't work with the Romanians. It was great when we were there, but when we were gone it was rubbish and nothing was taken on board and there was no follow-through. Even at that stage, before I went, I didn't believe that. I believed that the process was rubbish, not the country or the people of taking on board what was said.

I think a lot of people went out as trainers and educators who weren't trainers and educators. Who had trained them or educated them to culturally impart information in another language, in another culture, in another place? And I think people took a little bit of liberty, because there was no person saying, 'Stop, I'm not ready for this, I want to take it at this pace.' So the volunteers had the freedom to take it at their pace and then they felt what they did was wonderful and what the Romanians did was useless. And in any therapeutic relationship, that's not how I've been trained to work. We work in partnership and in pace with people and you give them as much as they can take on board or as much as they are asking for at the particular time. So I was much more interested in working in a place that was going to allow me to do process rather than product.

So over the period of maybe fourteen, fifteen years, the Tanners had children with profound disabilities living in group homes from Nicoresti orphanage. And at that time, they wanted me to be an occupational therapist and they wanted occupational therapy advice at that time of what to do. So for the first six months, my sole attention was eight children. You show the children what they need to do, you show the staff what they need to do and then you step back. That is my whole ethos with occupational therapy; you are surplus to requirement.

So already I was on side with the children, but I knew that that wasn't enough. That was not enough for me; that is not why I was there. I had made it clear if I was coming the carers must be there to see everything that I'm doing, otherwise there is no point. It is not our job for Romanian children to connect with a volunteer, they must connect with their caregivers and their foster parents. Otherwise it is even more hell for the children, that they have this activity for a time and then it is put away and they never see it again.

The first three months were really difficult. And they were difficult, because of a lot of miscommunication, no language, asking the carers to do really hard things with the children. Fear – because they were working with severely, profoundly disabled children and they had no training. They are local people; there was a lot of fear of hurting, actually hurting the children, or making the children sick. And they hated it. I think for them it was such a big shift that they probably fought with every volunteer that went, but in any relationship there has to be a little bit of persistence.

It was hard getting to grips with what they found challenging. When you don't have the language, what is it? Is it they don't like the children? Is it they don't like me? Is it they don't like me with the children? Is it they don't like volunteers? Is it they don't like Irish people? Is it they think we don't like them? Is it that we think they're not capable and why are we coming? Is it the rich/poor thing as well?

The house was new, the washing machine, the dryer were – these were new things to the local girls, you know. And they loved cleaning. They loved cleaning more than they loved minding the children. The house was spanking

Koyla, who left Tarasiki *Internat* in 2010 and now lives independently in his flat in Belarus, thanks to the support of the Kenny family from Dublin. *Photo: Burren Chernobyl Project.*

brand new; they were proud of it. And you know, they had their chores that they had to do like any mother in the house. And I used to think, 'Can the washing not wait, can the floor not wait, can the whatever not wait?' I was twenty-seven. I didn't have children, I didn't have my own home. And in the ten years after that, I realised that they never will have a home like that. You know, the way they cleaned the oven and the fridge; they'll never have a fridge or an oven like that and they just respect everything in the house. I used to think, 'If they wash the children with the same dedication as they wash the oven, I'll be very happy.'

But I started to do more helping with the day-to-day chores to free them to do things. So I got to learn the roster on the wall and I watched. By watching them and knowing them and talking to them and them talking to me in the little bit of English, over time ... I didn't spend much time with Irish volunteers ... I wanted the Romanian experience so on my days off I went to other houses, I went for walks, I tried to connect with local people. It was very difficult in the village; they are very suspicious of foreigners. You're a little bit nervous as well, of going into poverty or intruding on people. But bit by bit I tried to be available to the Romanians more so than be available to the volunteers.

I think the foreign volunteers just highlighted all the opportunities and things that they might never have, you know. The money and the materialism, those kind of things, you know, girls their age that were swanning off for pizza or into town or into the Internet cafes. And they had phones and they could call a taxi from the house anytime they wanted to go into town, which was twenty miles away. Go on their trips to Brasov or to the mountains or to the seaside or go on little day trips. But I didn't like those things personally … I did one or two trips, but I didn't feel comfortable doing that. I found I very much preferred to stay, to try to get to know where I was at. I didn't want to be a tourist.

And after the first six months I took a break for three weeks and came home and that was on advice at the beginning. That three-week break was absolutely key and crucial, because I asked for the next six months that I didn't go back with the title occupational therapist, but I went back with the title of carer; I no longer worked nine to four, I'd work eight to eight and I'd work nights and I'd work the same as the staff. And also, it wasn't helpful to have a title like that. Nobody has an OT seven days a week living in their home.

I know at the start things were very hard for the carers. So I think, you know, they've come really, really full circle. Their level of respect for the children has surpassed even the things that I think about, because they've lived with them and connected with them now for seven, eight years; and they realise their pain and they know their journey and their story, and me going for a week or two weeks or three weeks now. Yes, I did the foundation for the year, but … how they deal with the day-to-day and how they touch the children is just lovely.

About twelve months ago the volunteer programme stopped for good. Because the children have become young adults, have got to a level where it is time to be independent. I think it stopped because some of the older children could articulate that they didn't particularly like it anymore. The things that they say: 'I'm no longer a baby.' There's a lot of people who took pictures because they knew they'd never be back, so they left a photo as a memento. So there's photos of lots of faces around the place and I found that this time, looking at that, I'm thinking I'm glad in a way that there's no volunteer programmes, because you can't do that forever. You can't travel and be a tourist in somebody's home forever with a volunteer programme and leave a picture that I was here and I was here and I was here, because it is not healthy after a while for the children, that they have to say goodbye so many times – they no longer as young adults want that.

When we went last, one of the children had passed away, so we were there just after the funeral. And for all the volunteers, I was struck, really, by the lack of connection. One of the children that volunteers had worked with had passed away. There was no cards, there was no flowers, there was no emails particularly. It saddened me at the time. People don't understand why I go back. Even people in similar work, they ask, 'What are you going to do?' People don't really understand that you're there as a support, as an advocate, because you can. Because you can just go and be and it's a privilege to go there and be and say, 'I remember you when you were five' or 'I remember you when you were ten', to show them the albums and to look over things.

It wouldn't be fair to bring in really young kids now into a house full of young adults, young teenagers. Every house had an age span – it is funny how that happened – and had peers. So to bring in younger children now wouldn't be the way and I don't think that they [the Tanners] foresee that. They'd like to think that younger children are being provided for and supported in their own families and things like that. You know, the orphanage in Nicoresti is gone. The needs there have gone, have changed. There are no orphans in Nicoresti, but I'm sure they often get asked by Child Protection if they've got any space. But they are trying to move people on rather than fill beds.

And I think it is a great vision, you know. There was a decision made that when Casa Hannah was built, that was it, that there was going to be no more houses built. Could've had another couple of houses easily in the village, but the ideal was always to have a really high standard of care and quality of care for the children and you have to come to a point as a service of having a cut-off point. Otherwise the standard definitely will drop. You see the life progression having worked there for eight years and you see the problems with teenagers and the different work all the time to get things right and even to sit with one child and help them with homework and to help different people with different things ... it is definitely a challenge as it is. I really think it is like a family model. You have a set number of children and then you stop and you rear them. Whereas with an institution, you just keep having more and more and more.

'Find people who will work with you'

–Herbert Armitage & Noel Deane

Herbert (64) is the Chairperson of the national charity **Friends of the Children of Chernobyl**, which was set up in 1992 to bring children to Ireland for rest and recuperation holidays. The organisation has eleven local branches across Ireland. Noel (65) is the Chairperson of the Cloughjordan branch of Friends of the Children of Chernobyl since 1995.

> The interpreters we have we know well. For instance, I was introduced to Oksana by another interpreter, Angelica, who's married down in Galway. She introduced me to Oksana, and Angelica told me she is very good, very trustworthy. She'll work for you, work with you. We've never had a complaint about her, same as Angelica, we've never had any complaints about her either. Maybe it is just that we're lucky, but I usually tell the interpreter from the word go what we expect and what we don't expect, you know. We have a lot of trust in the interpreters.   *Noel Deane*

Herbert: The purpose of the group was to bring the kids over … We do other things now as well, but that would have been the main purpose, I think, of nearly any group set up to begin with, was to bring kids, get them out of the radiation. You know, I suppose we'd say because we have so many groups we look like we were bringing lot of kids where in reality it's small

Belarusian child enjoying a rest and recuperation holiday in Cloughjordan, Co. Tipperary. *Photo: Friends of the Children of Chernobyl.*

groups bringing small numbers of kids. We brought last year – between children interpreters or whatever – we brought approximately 220, 230 people. We brought them, and still bring them from schools. We've never worked in orphanages, there's plenty of people working in orphanages … you go out to villages … and there are still villages there where children have never come out.

Noel: We tried. We asked our host families here a number of years back to know whether they'd take kids from orphanages and they said no. Because it's not that we don't want to; it's giving back a child is their biggest problem – for the fact that the child will be going back into what it came out of. You're sort of teasing the child, 'Look at what you could have.' So we said, 'Okay, we'll stay away from orphanages.'

It's to give the children a month of clean air, good food and an enjoyable holiday. Because otherwise they'd be at home and they'd be in the field, or they'd be on the farm doing something like, it's not great for a child to be working all the time. You know, it's a good experience for them, but give them a break too.

There'd be a lot of people doing that, a lot of people that bring them. And a lot of people bring back the same child for years and years. We find that pointless, you're depriving another child of a bit of a holiday by bringing the same child back that often. Now if the child is an invalid ... we brought an invalid child back three times for – not necessarily medical reasons, but for health reasons, for food and for air, and we decided he needs it. So we bring him, you know. And as well as that, to give the mother a break, because they had, I think it was, three kids at the time, and 95 per cent of her time was taken up with the little fellow. So we said, 'Here we'll give her a break and what not, it's not going to break anybody.'

Host families here ask me what it's all about. I say, 'Listen, just do it and you'll be rewarded.' The feeling you get is absolutely super. A month is a long time and you'll look forward so much to them coming and again when the month is out, you'll look forward to them going back. But the feeling you get, you get a great feeling after doing something good and you think about other people; you're not thinking about yourself all the time. We have full and plenty; even in the recession we have full and plenty, we're not going to starve.

Herbert: We would go out to the schools and we would normally take a certain class at the school; we would go back to the same schools every year. We're working in about twenty-five schools now. It is a big operation I suppose, but you know once you get into the hang of it, it works along handy enough. We have a good relationship with the schools ... I'll personally have a good relationship with quite a lot of families, because I've met them.

You will meet them again and again in the school, if the family has three or four kids then you know next year, the year after, you meet them. I try and let them see we're just human, I try to have a bit of a joke. I'd be asking the kids where they think they're flying to, and what they think, and what are the things that come to mind? There's a map of the world on the wall and we asked the kids could they show me where Ireland was and they were all looking and were looking and they couldn't find it, and then the teacher pointed out this little dot and they all started to laugh. I asked them why they were laughing; they said, 'We're afraid to fall off into the water.' They begin to realise, you know, they're going to humans. You would see a big difference there if you go to a new school where children have never been out before, and the parents would be questioning you very seriously about it. You go back to that school the next year and you have a new set of parents with a totally different attitude, they'll have heard how the kids got on and you know that the thing is well run and all the rest of it.

I mean it's been marvellous, you know. I'm at the stage now – particularly in Luninets, which is a comparably small town – that people will actually stop you in the street and talk to you, know who you are, things like that. They're very, very welcoming people, they're lovely, friendly people, and their big thing is if you go to their house a big meal is put on, very often the meal that they can't really afford.

I remember a lady last year standing up in the classroom and I thought it was so brave of her. She had 3 or 4 kids and she had no husband and for some years one of our groups has been putting money for food … you know a box of food once a week … And she stood up in the classroom in front of all the other people in the village and thanked us for it. I thought, 'How hard was it for her to stand up and do that?' You know … they do appreciate it.

Noel: There is a huge amount of poverty. I know people will tell you that we have poverty in our own country, but we haven't – well, up to now it wasn't a poor country – and you have neighbours here that won't see you starve anyway. But they're a different breed of people over there. If you haven't got it, you can do without it. We support a number of families. We buy them different things, for example if they're in need of beds or food.

Herbert: I think part of the thing that works is we have a good network of interpreters who, to a certain degree, keep their eyes open. You know, I mean you need to know someone over there who knows what's going on, knows where the problems are. If you don't have someone like that you are going over into a kind of limbo, you know, where you don't really know … If you have someone say to you, 'This is a problem here, there is a problem there, maybe you'd like to get involved with this', then you know going over what you're going to do. Otherwise you're coming back before you discover that these things exist.

Noel: The interpreters we have we know well. For instance, I was introduced to Oksana by another interpreter, Angelica, who's married down in Galway. She introduced me to Oksana, and Angelica told me she is very good, very trustworthy. She'll work for you, work with you. We've never had a complaint about her, same as Angelica, we've never had any complaints about her either. Maybe it is just that we're lucky, but I usually tell the interpreter from the word go what we expect and what we don't expect, you know. Do your work and work for us, with us, and we'll treat you right and we do. We treat them right. There's enough looking for good causes without paying for a bad one. If there's somebody looking for help, like the hospital, or the school that we go to, or the lyceum, or any of them, the interpreters will tell us straight up whether that's a good person or that's a good man … We have a lot of trust in the interpreters. You have to have the word of mouth; it is better than the authorities.

I think the invalid children are more in need of a holiday than the school children in some ways. Children that are not going to an orphanage; children that are not taken into a day care centre; that are out in the middle of the sticks … children at home. I know it's twice as expensive to bring invalid children, because you have to bring the mother with them, but we get the host families here that look after them.

We had a young lad over here this year and he was okay until he had an operation on his back. And then he couldn't walk. He hadn't been out for six months; out of his apartment. Eight flights of stairs like, who was going to bring him out? Not the mother. So it's kids like that … they need it. For a break and to give the mother a break as well. To let both have a break and let them see there's more to life than this, than just sitting in the bloody apartment. Then the mother would have a holiday too, because the host family would help her.

It so happened that it was the father that came with him, because he was so big and heavy, the mother wouldn't have been able to look after him; lift him in or out. He had a whale of a time, he had a fantastic time. The host family he was with, they took the dad to the pub a couple of times. He drank Guinness; he'd never drank Guinness in his life. But yeah, he says, 'It's something I'll remember for the rest of my life' – when you hear a man saying that like, you know it means something …

Some of them now will visit when we go over in spring. And the smile on their face when they see you … So they'll invite you back to their house, which more often than not you can't go anyway, but if you do go back to their house, the child is let out of school there and then, and when you go to the house, there's a spread on the table, man alive. And the photographs are on the table, you know. It's a great experience for them and they're king of the castle for a length of time when they go back, because they're: 'I've been to Ireland and I've done this and I've done that.'

If you ask any of them, 'The best month of my lifetime, I can remember, was in Ireland.' Some of them will never leave their country and more of them ... the clever ones can't wait to get out. The kids going back have great memories; they'll tell you they have great memories. Things like that, that shows you that they appreciate what you did, they appreciate the holiday. The experience that they had, you know.

There on our fifteenth year they had a celebration for us. There was a concert held for us in Luninets and the whole place was done in Irish colours and 'Friends of the Children of Chernobyl' all over the place. And this concert was so long, God bless them. The Belarusian opera type of thing. We listen to music, sit there for hours listening to this and you're not knowing what was going on. But then they made all those presentations to myself and a couple more group leaders that were there. And it was good like, it showed that they appreciate what you do as well, you know. It was good, it was good.

The future, I hope it will keep going. All we can do is our best and after that, who knows? But there will always be groups. There will be groups that will be doing something, you know. I'd like to see that Chernobyl is not just forgotten. I don't think it will be forgotten. We're not looking for glory ... we just want it recognised that something is being done by outsiders. They can't understand how we're meant to do this. They think our government is at the back of it and helping them; helping us to help them. We do have to explain to them that our government doesn't even know we're here. They don't know we exist. That it's the ordinary, everyday people like yourselves that gives us money to give to you to help you.

Herbert: There are some groups have dropped out, there are a few others that have come in, you know, I suppose at this stage there are not going to be too many new groups formed for Chernobyl, it's an old cause ... and it's not flavour of the month anymore; you hear about Pakistan, everyone wants to give money to Pakistan. There's not really new groups as such coming in. You know, you feel good after, when the kids have gone back you feel you've done something worthwhile. It becomes part of your life.

'If you want to change things you have to stay in the equation'

– Conor Hughes

Conor (44) lives in Blackrock, Co. Louth, where he owns a music shop. He became involved in Romania in the late 1990s and set up **Cross Cause** in 2003 to work in Romania and Ghana. Cross Cause provides funding for a variety of projects, including residential services for children with disabilities in Romania.

> In particular, Romania is a country where you certainly learn patience, and I suppose you learn not to be a hot head. Lots of things will drive you mad; not necessarily in Romania, I'm sure in any of the eastern countries. But if you want to change things you have to stay in the equation, by fighting or pulling your outside circle, where there is a possibility of a solution, always to stay calm and to stick with it and then maybe you get a solution. The other way you get nothing.

I was always doing fundraisers for different charities – it was sort of a pattern I had got into and eventually I felt maybe I was at the point in my own life that I could actually, instead of giving the money away, I could see the money through, right to the end. This was something that was always a big issue with me – I would get this money off people for doing something and I'd hand it to some organisation and that was the end of my story with the money. I kind of fancied knowing more ... so that was the first sort of thought in my head.

I had no particular connection with Romania, I had no friends who'd been there or anything. Just in a logical way, I remember thinking, well, the European mainland would be good, because I bet I could bring goods. I thought it would be somewhere where you could physically take donations.

So that sort of pointed me towards Romania, and then I began asking around and doing a bit of nosing and investigation. I happened upon the orphanage in Nicoresti for kids with disabilities and was working there for a small amount of time, and then I continued slowly but surely. Even now I'm still learning things and I'm still making mistakes, but for sure I went out very naïve with a head full of ideas which all proved to be incorrect. But I learned my trade and as I learned I started to work out, I suppose, where I would be more use. I'm a shopkeeper, you know I'm not in the care society or trained in anything, to be honest; I'm a shopkeeper.

One thing I did spot immediately was that pouring of goods and love into the government institutions was wasteful. I had seen that within a very short amount of time, and I have seen so many truckloads of stuff being poured in the front door of an orphanage and within weeks leaving by the back door and it barely having any effect on the youngsters. Lots of people will recognise themselves in this story, I'm sure. I can remember one particular time where we brought over a quantity of 'Christy Moore on Tour' T-shirts and they had been printed wrong, the dates were wrong, so we got them. We were very pleased giving them out and putting them on all the kids. Slowly but surely they started making their way into the village as expected, and then they made their way to the town eleven miles away, so they were travelling quite far, until one of our volunteers was in Bucharest four hours away and saw people wearing them there too, and one particular lady got fed up with this. She went down to the local police station to complain about this, only to be met at the door by a policeman wearing a 'Christy Moore on Tour' T-shirt. So that was, I guess, an anecdotal statement of what was occurring.

Really, the best thing I was doing was learning and watching and seeing where I could be useful. So I started asking, am I more use just carrying stuff out to the country or could I do more than that? Within two years, myself and a few of the other volunteers that I connected with had decided we would buy our own house and transfer the most vulnerable youngsters from the orphanage into that house and that's what we did. We did it very quick, we bought our first small rural house and immediately brought a team over from

Children and Irish volunteers outside Buchemble Orphanage in Belarus (2010). *Photo: Chernobyl Orphans Fund.*

Ireland then to convert the house. We were actually the laughing stock of the village, because in January we were doing this, when cement doesn't even dry, so we were lighting fires to make the cement dry and they thought we were all crazy. We were so energised with what we wanted to do there was nothing going to stop us, no elements or no uncomfortableness, and we managed it and by March we had a fine house and we moved our first three girls into it.

Casa Bridget is the name of the first house we built; so when we got that, then within a year or so we expanded it and then we built a big wing and then we built another addition and then we bought the property next door, so we just kept buying next door, we were obsessed with over our garden gate, you know, a neighbour who has designs on his neighbour's property, that's what we were like … I suppose we got greedy, for want of a better word. It must be just people, mankind, that they always want to do bigger and better, whether it be financially or emotionally, in every statement you want a car, you want a bigger one; but certainly when we got the one kid, then the two kids and three kids, we wanted more.

We are official and get some aid locally, we get a salary for carers and the kids, the young adults receive a pension. So it's something towards our budget. A big part of the monthly spend would be salaries for the staff in the house, the care system we have in the village and then we employ a couple of social workers for the greater community and their job really is to keep an eye on the village, to see particularly bad cases and bring it to our attention to see if we can do anything. One great ongoing thing which social workers do for us is they find people who never had a pension, never applied for the pension, maybe an elderly person or someone caring for their own special needs child and never got a pension for them.

We build these little houses for poor families in the community. We bought a plot just along the road from us and built there. We have eighteen of them now. Poor families from the village. Families that are eager to get on and have, even in their poor circumstances, maybe great effort to keep their kids clean and get them to school. We always identified ones that, given a fresh start with a nice house and electricity and running water … yes, the deal is they are in them now and they are built two and a half, three years now, they will own them in five years if they mind them, and so far there is only one family who still have to prove themselves. Everybody else has developed the house – they have all built lean-tos at the back for their agriculture and are doing a really great job so that they have been a success, and the reward is five years and they will own the houses. So this is all based in Nicoresti village.

All the emotions come out, because you're giving to others and rejecting others and so … jealousy comes up quite a lot. Then the reverse of people loving you because you have done something for them. You try not to show favouritism and you don't want to be the big Westerners throwing your money around, so we try and keep a level of fairness towards everybody and try and help maybe to try and do things that would affect everybody. We've helped the local schools and things, so that should affect everybody in the community and they will have got something out of it. There are quite a few people in the village employed, but you are still an alien, you're always an alien, you're always this bizarre Westerner that people have come up with all sorts of reasons why you're there, you know, and I'm sure lots of people are suspicious of our reasons, you know, are they making money out of it? I remember at the start when we came to the institution, one of them said,

'Did you commit crimes in Ireland that this is your punishment?' Instead of being sent to prison in Ireland, we were sent to Romania.

I've learned an awful lot, because I suppose I've been in every aspect of the project, you know, from loading trucks to site, to dealing with the authorities on the other side. Because of that, I have learned a lot. I suppose patience is one thing for sure. In particular, Romania is a country where you certainly learn patience, and I suppose you learn not to be a hot head, because lots of things will drive you mad; not necessarily in Romania, I'm sure in any of the eastern countries where authorities are not going your way and people really don't see things. But if you want to change things you have to stay in the equation, by fighting or pulling your outside circle, where there is a possibility of a solution, always to stay calm and to stick with it and then maybe you get a solution. The other way you get nothing.

A few years ago, the orphanage where we were working closed all of a sudden, and overnight they all moved across towards the Moldovan border. We had all these high hopes when they moved over, we didn't realise what the conditions were and it turned out to be another travesty. So from then on we started working with the new director; myself, I struck a good relationship with her. She is nice and she let us buy them a lot of things and we keep in with her and get the balance right, you know, keep a good relationship. You know, it's very easy to go in and start criticising and going crazy and you get nothing out of them, they just say you would be barred from us and then what good are you? So you have to be diplomatic. I suppose you have to sometimes allow seeing something that is not particularly appealing. You might have to let it go by for the greater good of keeping the relationship good. Because we've had it that maybe a volunteer went down and emotions got carried away and we got thrown out because of that and I would have to go down and sweet talk them and praise them. But it was really important to get that relationship right, and in our case we could lift a phone and say we are coming down anytime.

The thoughts of people giving you money and you 2,000 miles away just wasting it with bad decisions is a good driving force for you to be careful. It was back to the fact that I'd been given this huge position of trust where people gave me money and without saying anything they'd allowed me to make the decisions of where to spend it, to trust me. That's a rare position to occupy in the world – who does that? People give you money in exchange for your work or goods, but no one gives you money and says, 'Do what you can with that.' At the very start, when I started being given money to do this, that was when I had to decide, right, I'm not going to pour it in the front door of an orphanage; even though I want to do my best for the youngsters there, there is a better way of doing it. So that was a slow process, to find which was the best way of doing it. I suppose to impact on the most people for the least amount of money.

I'm quite a commercial thinker, I always think somewhat in the business line, because getting money from people is kind of what a businessman is, that's what he does, he extracts money for goods; in this particular case, the goods or the product is a charity. I think for a long time there we were kind of in the shade. It seems like we're all courting people to praise us, but it's not like that; but I did discover, I think, it's much better for a charity to have a high profile – you just get more money. As much as it's nice to be coy and silent than not courting praise, you get more money from the commercial world by letting people know what you're doing. We've become a lot more visible now. We've got a shop now and we've logos and all the paraphernalia of a business, really, and it worked. It's just been practical.

The Cross Cause logo is written like little people, and the little people are pushing a reluctant elephant up a hill. And from the second day I landed in Romania, my whole image of the place was that it was like: push the workers, like pushing an elephant up a hill. It doesn't particularly want to go up, and if you take the pressure off at all it will roll down and trample you. I don't see any let up in the necessity to be pushing, but that's fine. Once you've accepted that you get on with it.

It's who I am now. If I stopped being involved – I suppose this isn't just some evening class that I do, this is what I do. And apart from the obvious thing like the results and the sense of wellbeing that you get from doing something ... one real interesting by-product from it is you spend most of your time surrounded with brilliant people, really good people, so most of my day is spent from amongst Cross Cause volunteers and friends of the charity. Amongst really decent people. In life, that's an ambition everybody should have, you know, the positive thinkers are always eager to help and people who can endure if it means a better life for other people, and they are the people I spend my days with, so that's a great reason to continue.

'There has to be give and take'
–Ned Hayden & Brian O'Sullivan

Ned (61) is a Christian Brother and a retired teacher living in Cork. Brian (26) is a qualified nurse and occupational therapy student who now coordinates a volunteer medical programme for **Burren Chernobyl Project**. Both are board members of the charity, which supports children and adults with disabilities in institutions and communities in Belarus.

> There's probably a lot of negotiation. I think in general, any kind of relationship, over time you'd hope that it would get a lot stronger and that you'd get closer from both sides. Then again, change is never easy for anyone. You are doing something. They don't really like it. You are introducing all of these new ideas. Saying to operate on a child when he is perfectly fine sitting there. You have to tell them that he isn't fine sitting there. *Brian O'Sullivan*

Ned: It was when I was teaching in Ennistymon I first became aware of the Chernobyl kids. The place where we were living, we had a few extra rooms, so a number of kids came over around '97-'98 … kids with disabilities would have come over and stayed in the house. Yeah, I remember the first couple of years being there and they'd be in around the place and they'd be coming in the kitchen and I'd be shouting for somebody, 'Come in and take this fellow away!' Oh, it was … I definitely didn't feel happy with them. I just wanted them away from me. These were different.

But a few of the women up around Ennistymon said, 'Look, you have to come out, you must come out.' I suppose around '98 was the first time I would have gone out to Cherven *internat* [boarding institution], and it definitely was a major thing. I remember three times going into Cherven and kind of having to come out, because the smell was dreadful. The smell of people who were just lying in cots, the place dark and miserable, just lying there in faeces and a fair amount of it around them. And carers, they were there kind of standing and accepting this as the norm, or this is the way things were here. Absolutely dreadful situation – you were in the bed, you were there and that was it.

I had no idea about disability. Well, I would have seen people with disability, but I never had to deal with them. And people with disabilities wouldn't have been in schools at that stage. A few people here and there in wheelchairs, but I mean the people I would have met in wheelchairs, okay, they were in wheelchairs, but in every other way they were intelligent, they were fine, they were in school, they were coping in school. Whereas here they were confined to bed, they couldn't move.

You know, once you're there though ... I felt there was something I could do. Okay, I could wash them or clean them or feed them. And feeding them was a bit of a disaster, I wasn't used to it, some of them were quite good at it. I'd be rather slow, but still, you felt you were doing something. Like trying to feed them sitting up, a fair amount of it came out again, because they weren't used to eating that way, but at the same time it seemed not very nice feeding them lying down and you were just spooning in stuff and it was just disappearing.

I remember two brothers there, they were seventeen and they had been in there, put in from the age of seven and put into cots. And this was ten years later and they were still in the same cots. So they had grown up, you see, so all their limbs, their legs in particular, had grown up back under them, or grown off at the side that just had to fit within the size of this seven-year-old's cot. So there was dirt and muck of basically ten years all over them and all around them, and I remember cleaning them or helping people to clean them and they just smiled at you. And trying to get the dirt out from behind legs that were buckled up and things and they still smiled. And I mean, it must have been extremely painful, but they just smiled. The biggest thing I would've learned from that was that I thought I had difficulties or problems here, but it's nothing compared to what they were suffering or going through and still, all they could do was smile. Does your pain threshold grow according to the way you are treated? I don't know. Hopefully it did for them.

As well, after a while they became individuals and you would see individual personalities, they became individuals in their own right; whereas when you walked in first they were just a whole room full of people lying in the bed. So taking them out, helping them to walk, that kind of thing, you know – it was what was there in front of you, so you dealt with what was there. I wouldn't have dealt with it over here. When you go out, as I said, five, six years, you become friends with the people. And you want to go back and see how they are, how they're doing, have they improved, have they got worse. Some of them can go way downhill, some of them can be a lot better. You just like to be with them and you feel things are improving.

Brian: I think it was going there the first time that I realised that something had to be done. I think the severity of how bad things are affects you. Disability is really profound. In Goradishche orphanage, there is one group that you say, 'Jesus, Mary and Joseph, how could things be so bad?' That was the first impression. I remember leaving it and I couldn't get it out of my head no matter how hard I tried. There was just an image running around. That is literally what it is … just people lying there and just waiting. There's nothing happening for them. I just felt that it could be so much more. I think that first experience had a huge impact on me. I think you can either look at it two ways: you see the situation and say nothing is improving here, or you can say, 'This is not impossible to change.' I think that change is possible. We are all open to change.

I probably approach every situation differently now. It is a learning curve. I think sometimes when people come out who are working in disability services here, they find it difficult, they are coming to their boiling point, they're frustrated. You just have to step back and try and put it in context. I think that no matter how much people try and tell you, this is something that you have to find out yourself. It's a learning game, because you're trying to work with all these people, and this has been huge for me, because this isn't my background. I have a degree in nursing. We are taking things to a whole new level. We are trying to coordinate volunteers and orientate them and do up all these programmes. You have to start performing, you have to start getting this right.

The biggest barrier is attitude to disability. Attitude, I think … maybe not just attitude on the ground level, but attitude at the government level. It's changing … it has changed in five years. There are more disability acts coming in. They are putting more day care centres in place. They are acknowledging it slowly. We have to be patient with it, because if it was ten years ago, it wouldn't have happened. They are coming on board … even some of the government officials. They have been travelling. They've been here … they've been there. They aren't just working from their own mindset. They are travelling to other European countries and looking to how things are being done there and how they are managing the situation there. For the most part, I think they are happy to work with us. It's just about us breaking down those barriers, and saying that there is no reason why this child can't come in, or this child deserves a place in here.

There's probably a lot of negotiation. I think in general, with any kind of relationship, over time you'd hope that it would get a lot stronger and that you'd get closer from both sides. Then again, change is never easy for anyone. You are doing something. They don't really like it. You are introducing all of these new ideas. Saying to operate on a child when he is perfectly fine sitting there. You have to tell them that he isn't fine sitting there. It probably pi**** them off. I know some people in the orphanage and they aren't happy with me. However, I think when they see the same faces coming back and the relationship builds … the same people over time, it's easier for them. Volunteers have to work in parallel, on the same level as them. It must be very hard for them to think that these people are walking in here for two weeks and they think they are professionals and then after two weeks, they are gone. We are the ones carrying the can. It's just that we work very much at the same level as them. We just involve them as much as we can.

Over time when you go back you gradually find ways of working with them and taking their point of view on board. There are many different ways of approaching it. You could take the very laid back approach and say it's going to happen in time. But then you have to look at it at some time and say, 'Look, this child needs to be fed properly. We aren't in here for the fun. We are bringing over people. We are doing this for a reason. You need to start getting in behind us.' It's the same with the community; one guy I know out there was involved in a traffic car accident, with a spinal cord injury. You can go in there and people can keep saying, 'Poor Sasha isn't it awful for you?'

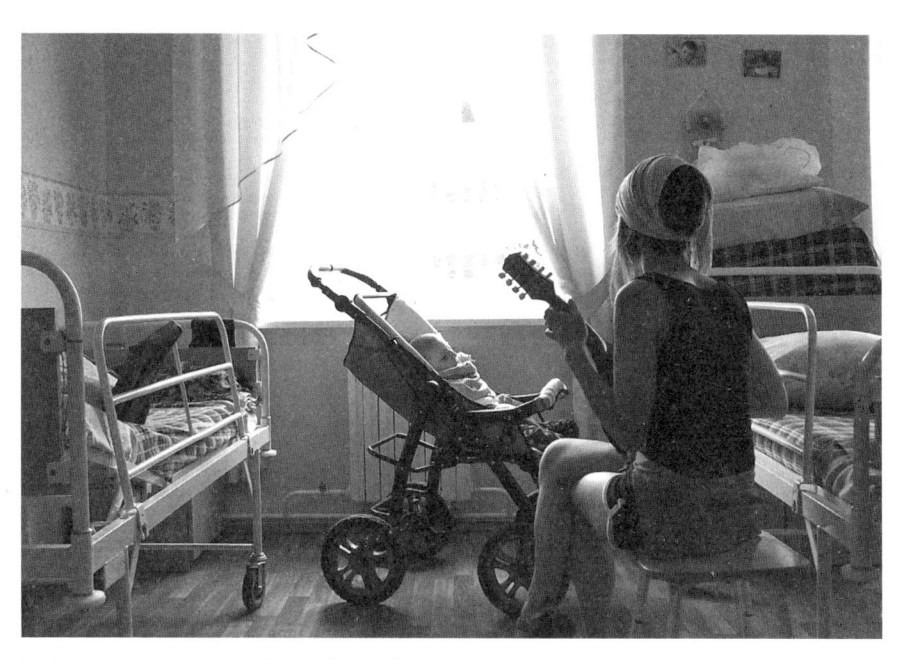

Irish volunteer singing to Nikita from Cherven *Internat* for children with disabilities in Belarus (2010). *Photo: Maurice Gunning/Burren Chernobyl Project.*

He can keep saying, 'Poor me, poor me.' We say you need to start pulling yourself together here; you have to start getting behind this. You need to start coming on board, because you do have potential. Maybe life isn't going to be what it was like five years ago, but things can certainly get an awful lot better. It's probably the same as here. You can be overly sympathetic at times. There has to be give and take. At times, you just have to give them a kick in the a** and say, 'Get on board.' In general, there is a good relationship. There has to be.

The Irish wouldn't be there twenty-five years on if there wasn't. There is a huge commitment among the Irish. Maybe it's just the Irish as a whole in every place they are involved in. I think that when they get into something, they are really behind it. I think the Irish aren't just there in terms of finance, but they are on the ground. When you are at the airport, you meet the Irish going over and back. There isn't a flight that you are on that there aren't any Irish people. There are a lot of dedicated people.

Ned: I suppose we would have learned a lot about volunteers. You need to give them a fair idea before they go out of what to expect. The other thing that we found very important, even more important, was meeting people when they come back. And part of that would be, say, I come back and I meet my friends and they ask me about it or something and I start talking about it. To a great extent they are not terribly interested, it's outside their understanding. Not that they don't have sympathy for you, but basically what they'd say is: 'Aren't you great? Oh, isn't that marvellous? Aren't you terrific?' And you feel anything but. You feel to a certain extent privileged to have been out, but there's a kind of, though ... feeling of, 'I need to do some more.' But more often than not what you need is just somebody to listen to them and very often we find that somebody more or less their own age would be better.

Brian: I think it pays off to look after volunteers, to make sure that they are properly looked after. I think young people of any background are incredible in the way that they can face it. People often criticise youth for being lazy or whatever. I think it's a huge advantage to get young people involved and getting students involved, but I think you need to get them out there. It's just giving Burren Chernobyl a new way of looking at things. For a long time, the charity was running on a day-to-day basis. We are here today and we'll be here tomorrow and hopefully we'll be there the day after next. People had to take a step back and say, 'We are hoping to be here in ten years time. If we want to be here in ten years time, how are we going to go about it? What do we need to do?' Improving our website, tapping into the Bebos and Facebooks and everything else like that.

We are pulling in new volunteers and we aren't just tapping the same resources. We should be recruiting people nationwide, keeping these people involved. I suppose for that to happen, the volunteer needs to feel that it's worth it to involve your colleagues. There's no point in people saying this is a waste of time, because nothing was in place when we went over. People have become more professional in recent years, especially around volunteering. They want to be treated with professionalism. From our side, we have to make sure that that is happening.

Recently we've set up a local charity, Dobra Tut – it is the child of Burren Chernobyl in Belarus. So, in terms of accountability, it makes it easier for purchasing houses and running funds from Ireland to Belarus and monitoring where the humanitarian aid goes. It's easier working through the Department of Humanitarian Aid in Belarus when you have a Belarusian charity. In terms of volunteering, involving Belarusians, it's easier when they associate it with a Belarusian charity. They are trying to break down the barriers in Belarus ... just involving people and encouraging volunteering and funding from Belarus. One of the staff even organised the first Belarusian rock concert and they got Belarusian rock bands and they did an event for Burren Chernobyl. It might be four or five hundred in attendance ... which might be small. But for Belarus, it's very big. Finding new ways and creative ways of catching their attention ... finding a way of relating. Get them involved in it ... All our work would be funded through Burren Chernobyl at the moment. In time, as they start to make more of an awareness in Belarus, hopefully a small degree will be funded from the community, from the Belarusians themselves.

There may be a degree of challenge, but saying that, there's always a way to change. It's just to believe in it, to really, really believe in it. Maybe there has to be an aspect of a politician in you at times, that you are really pushing it and to really have a belief in it. It did have a huge impact on me. Every month of the year, I seemed have been involved with Belarus. I think it's easy to get more involved when there are more people with you on the journey.

'Focus on what you're good at'
–Stuart Wilson

Stuart (41) is a psychotherapist from Dublin who became involved in the region in 1995 organising short term mission trips. He set up **Zest4Kidz** with his wife Maggie in 2004, to help support child soldiers, children involved in prostitution and children in prison in Belarus, Georgia, Uganda and India.

> **I mean for us, I think as well it's very important to know – what are we actually good at ... and try and focus on what you're good at. What do we do and do well? And for us we know what that is. You can end up having an organisation trying to be what they're not and not do it very well and I think that can, long term, be more damaging.**

I just wasn't expecting to see what I saw out there. You know, one of the first orphanages I saw in Belarus in 1995, it was minus twenty-five degrees, there were no panes of glass in the windows in those days, and the kids were eating off the floor. And I just came out of the place probably more angry than I've ever been in my entire life. The kids shouldn't be treated that way. I said, 'I can change this.' Then we got involved and I just kept travelling out, kept going, kept going ...

After that I travelled extensively in Eastern Europe, so everywhere from the former Soviet Bloc, to Romania, Georgia, Azerbaijan, and even into the Middle East as well, working in Afghanistan, Iran, Iraq ... There's certain places that really need help and then there's certain places that are in absolute bits. I suppose what we did, rather than go by country, was we actually selected categories of kids, and so we had child prisoners, children involved in prostitution and child soldiers – that's our gig, it's what we do. For me they were really forgotten kids, they were kids who no one was helping and no one was working with and we said well we'll step in.

My background is in psychotherapy and working with kids in Ireland with behavioural difficulties and with things like that, and I really wanted to try to help to see change in these kids' lives so that they weren't going back to the same things that got them in there in the first place. And I had worked in Ireland with the prison system, so I had some pretty successful programmes that we had run which had seen prisoners recuperated, rehabilitated and back into society and being part of society in a positive way again. And I wanted to try and see if we could run something similar in Eastern Europe. We feel this is what we're meant to be doing and not trying to be all things to all communities and all people.

I mean for us, I think as well it's very important to know what we are actually good at … and try and focus on what you're good at. What do we do and do well? And for us we know what that is. You can end up having an organisation trying to be what they're not and not do it very well and I think that can, long term, be more damaging.

I think it's very good to have a coordinated effort going into a region or going into an area and finding out what others do there and therefore what can we do that's different? What's our strengths that we can help with and can we work with another organisation who are in there? Maybe one who are in there helping to keep an orphanage heated and warm, but are the staff trained to work with young people? Because if the staff are happy, the kids are going to be happier.

So how can we help them first of all to make their lives better and what can we do for them? First of all it's about having a relationship with them and understanding their needs. It's about developing that over a period of time, you're not going to do it overnight. It's about having constant contact, it's about having backup programmes so if something goes wrong we're there to help. It's about being able to let the staff feel like they're of worth, they're cared for, and that they've got what it takes to be able to help the girls and the boys in these difficult institutions. It's about sometimes seeing that the staff are just grown up kids who have been through the same system.

We've had pretty serious success in one of the girls' prisons in Belarus, where they are not going back to the same things that got them in there. We work with them a year in advance of them leaving the prison and before they come out they're given the skills and the tools that they need to basically be able to adapt to society again. And the way that we've gone about doing that has been good, because we have worked ourselves with the girls in the prison, and developed a team of about ten girls who were previous prisoners who have left who are now the mentors to the girls who are in the prison.

And what I love now is that we're seeing the fruit of the seeds that we sowed back then, which is that those girls felt a connection, love and that family environment and that they want to stay and be a part of it. So they have gone on, some of them have had very successful marriages and have had babies and now they're still inputting into the girls in the prisons … Basically when you're in the prison you think you have no worth, you think you're useless, you think you have no place in society. So when they're feeding back into those girls they're doing it from a place saying I was here, I was here five years ago. And so that's powerful.

You need to ask what are your talents, what are you great at? What would you like to do with your life? People want to do it for themselves. They want to have standing within their community and we've seen people just come alive in the different programmes that we're involved with, because they've got such high self-esteem for themselves because they're doing it. They've got a job, they're supplying the needs of their family, they feel good. If you just get handouts, what's the point?

Irish people are great, but I think for many years, going into parts of Eastern Europe, we go in and we sing songs and we dance and we go around orphanages and we give out presents and then we leave. And that's it – we're gone. Happy Christmas and we leave. And I had a real problem with that – what about the rest of the year for these kids? It's great that we can give them a Christmas gift and I'm sure they won't get anything again; however, what about in January? What's going to happen to them? Not only that, but what about this kid who's not getting tucked in by anybody at bedtime and how's their emotional needs and who loves them? Who tells them that they're loved?

I think we can, as Irish people, think that we have the answers to Eastern European problems and we don't. We think we know what to do to make things better and we don't. The mistake we can make is go in and start handing out

Casa Sf. Iosif in Bucharest opened in September 2000 and now home to over 30 children from the streets. The centre also offers a day service to children who come for baths, clothing and food. *Photo: Street Children of Bucharest.*

stuff all over the place thinking, 'Let's make their environment better, let's make their houses look better, let's bring them up to Irish standards', and that's not something that has to be done. Unfortunately communism has had a way of, you know, being a very serious de-motivator in these countries so, I mean, the Eastern bloc has got a grayness attached to it which communism has brought in. And in many cases it's hard to lift that. So when I see our girls involved in uplifting and promoting and encouraging the younger girls in the prisons now in the same way we would have done, that's what's empowering, that's what's important.

A lot of it depends on our relationships, my personal relationship with them, my wife's and our in-country workers and coordinators and how they get on with the governors and staff. They're coming often from a background of the same difficulty as the kids. And I suppose we can forget about that and think it's all about the kids; in actual fact, one of the assistant governors, who is a wonderful woman, was in a horrendous car crash and we were able to help her through the difficulties that she had, laid on her back for six months, you know? So quite often it's relational, its developing a relationship so that you're trusted to the extent that they allow us to do the work.

Why we do it is an important thing to address all the time, because I think quite often we can as Irish people ... people want to help other people. We can do it because it makes us feel good or we can do it because we feel good and we just want to help other people – there's a big difference. My philosophy has always been: if you feel full you naturally spill over into other peoples lives, and I've always wanted it to be that way, rather than people coming on trips just to get a feel-good factor, but that they're full and they want to pass that on rather than the other way around.

'Everyone has a different skill'
–Jim McQuaid

Jim (59) is a retired school teacher from St Patrick's Grammar School in Armagh. He has been involved in **School Aid Romania** since 1993. The project is a cross-community initiative which brings teams of students to Brasov in Romania to deliver aid and funding.

> Another thing is, too, you should really have a team. You really can't do everything yourself. I am the leader of the week, but in many ways I'm only there to sort of rubber stamp things. Our team would consist of people who are very good at doing certain things that I, for example, wouldn't be good at. And that – I think that's very, very important. Because we all have good, possibly limited skills. There's not many people who would have all the necessary skills to do this sort of thing.

School Aid Romania itself began in 1990. It's a Northern Ireland-based cross-community charity, with two aims. The first aim is to bring together sixth form students, who would be sixteen-, seventeen-year-old students, in their second to last year of school, to bring them together and to be able to give them the opportunity to meet young people from another religion. People from the other side of the house, we would say up home. Our second aim is to help in Romania.

In 1993 our school was one of two pilot schools from the Armagh area who went out to Romania, and my son was one of six pupils who went out from our school, and six from another school. And when he came back, he said to me, 'Dad, if you ever get a chance, you should go.' So the next year the school decided to get fully involved, and we were sending out a group of about twelve students, with two other schools. One teacher was chosen to lead the group, and they were looking for one more volunteer. A number of us volunteered, and our names were just put in a hat and drawn out, and I happened to be the lucky one. So it was just a pure lottery. And really, I've been going ever since.

We work in the city of Brasov, and it's really only people from Northern Ireland who are still going there. The early days you'd have met a number of Germans, for example, who would have been there, and you would have met a number of Americans; but really nowadays you don't meet those people at all. And I have to say Brasov has now come on tremendously. I tell the students now, as they're driving into Brasov, it's like driving along into Malone Road in Belfast, you'll see the Mercedes garage, the Ford garage, the Peugeot garage, Carrefour supermarket, McDonalds. And you wonder: 'Why am I here?' But in saying that, a couple of days later they suddenly realise why they're there.

We visit everywhere, from the maternity hospital to the old people's home. We go to hospitals, clinics, orphanages, centres for the homeless. We work with street children, the Down's Syndrome centre, the school for the deaf. We go to a lot of institutions, all around Brasov. We go to the prison as well. The psychiatric hospital. We bring them cigarettes. A drink. Some biscuits. Some sweets, some fruit. You know, it's minimal. We are thanked to do that.

We would always go to an institution, every institution we've been to, we go with something. And we try to identify what needs they have. In the early days we would have imposed our thoughts on the people out there. We would have told them: 'You need this. We think you need this.' Nowadays we do it more in cooperation with them. And it's also in cooperation with our young people, because after all, they are the ones who have raised the money. And they're the ones who make the decision how to spend the money. The only time that I would step in is if they maybe identify something that they think to be a need, and maybe then if myself, or another adult, through experience of being there, we'd maybe realise that no, what the people are requesting might not be appropriate. Because we've had our fingers burnt in the years gone by, and we've bought things, and things have been misused, or they haven't been used in the institution, or they've maybe been sold on.

We've discovered that. So we try to keep a much tighter eye, and there are some people that we are very wary of dealing with. And we would just say to the young people: 'Look, we've bought that for them before, and it hasn't been a success.'

We sent out a couple of containers of aid in the early days. We stopped doing that then, because it was more hassle than it was worth. There was more hassle when you got out there, in terms of you were landing in a deprived country. You were unloading the stuff, you had to guard it. You also had the problem you were dependent on what people were giving you. Those early days, there were lots of things you couldn't buy; now we really just take money out with us. We take some limited medication that you can't get out there, would be difficult to get, but we really don't bring aid out anymore. We do a couple of food programmes in villages. We buy it out there, and that's another thing, we like to put money into the local community. Whereas we could get some stuff cheaper in the big supermarkets – and they do have big supermarkets and the big cash and carry places now – if we're in a village, we like to use the local shop. We like to warn them beforehand that we'll be there, we just don't want to clear everything out and leave nothing for the local people, so we tell them a number of days beforehand: 'We will be here, we will be buying for a hundred families', and they then would stock up. We don't want them to think, 'Oh, who are these people coming in, and supplying all the food, and then we have nothing to sell.' And I find if you do that, the locals work better with you.

The best way to help, I think, is to work with them. To encourage them to improve themselves. The idea of constantly just giving them something and walking away is not going to cure any problems. Encourage the cooperative idea, getting them to work at their own houses, and getting them to have a sense of their own community. And in truth, that's much, much better than simply bombing in, leaving a whole lot of aid, and blowing town. We just try to get them really to help themselves. But it's a slow process. And it's a process that has evolved, we didn't do that years ago.

Years ago we would have given what we thought was the appropriate aid, and maybe it wasn't. Now we work with people in the villages, and we'd get them to identify the poor that need help, and then we'd get them to identify what food we should buy for them. You know, their diets and our diets are completely different. They love oil. They must have used a lot of oil in their cooking, they love pasta and that type of thing, and those sort of sausage-y meat things, that we would tend not to eat here. And that's the sort of thing that we would buy for them. Maybe if we were going to go and do it, we would just go into a shop and buy the wrong food. We let them pick what they want.

We started working to try and do something for a local woman and her family, which was difficult – we did a building job using local labour in her house. What we said to them was: 'If everybody works here and helps build this lady's house, and if you, say – you men – help us do it, we then do your house or your house next, but everybody helps everybody else.' And that has been very successful. And they just move from house to house, and that can keep going on, really, forever. And we'll do up all the houses. We give them a cement mixer, and a block-making machine where they can make their own blocks.

Schools nowadays go out on trips to Africa. I've been out in Africa – I was doing a talk one day on poverty, out at a primary school, and I showed them a picture taken out in Africa, and we were talking about poverty and I asked them what it meant to be poor. So I showed a photo of this lady, in the Turkwel Desert in Kenya. I told them: 'That woman out there in the desert, she wasn't hungry. She didn't have a lot to eat, but she wasn't hungry.' She wasn't really deprived of anything. She didn't have anything, but she wasn't deprived. She wasn't cold. Nobody would have had a structured job or employment as such, there was no wage coming in, but there was no poverty, as defined by the United Nations.'

Whereas this other particular house, that I showed them the picture of in Romania, was the worst poverty I had ever seen, and that was only a couple of years ago. She had eight or nine children the first time I was there, and we gave them furniture, gave them beds, and in the wintertime she burned the beds for fuel. And she initially lived in a house with a hole in the roof, and they lived in one room. I have a picture of that, one night, and their dinner was potato skins. Now, potato skins are something you can get in any fancy restaurants in the area here. But these were potato skins – she didn't have the potatoes, they'd have been scavenged out of somebody's bin. And that's what they were going to have. I said to those kids, 'That's poverty.' Because they know there's a better life out there. That woman in Africa doesn't know. She has no concept of satellite TV, or how they live in New York or anything,

Students from Armagh delivering aid in Brasov, Romania. *Photo: School Aid Romania*

she's just living in her own little small desert area. They weren't poor, even though they had nothing. But those people in Romania were, because they were wet, and cold, and they were hungry, and they knew there was a better life out there.

Another thing is, too, you should really have a team. You really can't do everything yourself. I am the leader of the week, but in many ways I'm only there to sort of rubber stamp things. Our team would consist of people who are very good at doing certain things that I, for example, wouldn't be good at. And that – I think that's very, very important. Because we all have good, possibly limited skills. There's not many people who would have all the necessary skills to do this sort of thing. For example, we'd have people who are very good at record keeping … who'd be absolutely meticulous – and you must have somebody in your team who is good at doing that … because you're going to forget things. You're going to forget what you've bought, you're going to forget from day to day, week to week. So you must have somebody who's good at that.

Even down to something as simple as the first night we arrive at the hotel, the logistics of putting people into rooms. You're maybe given rooms that hold two, that hold three, that hold four. And you've got maybe thirty students, and you've got so many boys and so many girls. You need somebody who can simply just look at that, and we have somebody like that. It's their forte. They can do that, and that makes it very easy, when we arrive at the hotel. And the next day, when it comes to the shopping, we've got people who are excellent shoppers. And they're very good at allocating different people to do different things. Our students do the shopping, but we set them up into teams. We have some people who are very good at organising that sort of thing. Everybody has a different skill, and everybody uses that skill, I'm the leader, but there's no such thing as everything coming back to me. Everybody does their own thing, they do it independently, and we're lucky, it works. And the other weeks are the same. And what you find is, you build up a team and that team sticks together. So in my point of view, that's crucial to the success of the whole thing.

The cross-community element has worked exceptionally well. As you know, we've historically had trouble on the Garvaghy Road, with the impasse there. I've had people out from both sides of the community who would never, ever have met before. One who was trying to march down the Garvaghy Road, and one trying to stop them marching down. And they met. Yeah, it's lovely. And that's just a bond. It matures them tremendously. This has come to me from other schools as well. There are some who've been selected to go to Romania, and maybe have had a chequered past, and they have changed. You will find that.

Every year I sort of think: are we heading towards the end? You just don't know. We're subject to the schools. If the schools decided not to partake in the programme ... I have to say I just don't know. I would hate to see it ceasing to exist, but I would have predicted when Romania got into the European Community that it would have been down to its last few years, but all the time we're finding new – it's wrong to say problems – we're just finding new things to do all the time.

'Create self-sufficiency'
–Stephen Conway

Stephen (45) first became involved with Samaritan's Purse in 1999, while working as a self-employed decorator. He subsequently began working for the organisation as International Projects Coordinator in 2007. The organisation changed its name to **Team Hope** in 2010 and works in aid and development projects in over twenty-five countries, including Eastern Europe and the former Soviet Union.

> I think out of all the things that I have learned, certainly one of the most important things for me would be to set up anything so that when we leave, it keeps going ... it's self-sufficient. Whether that's an education programme where people continue to go to school and get educated after we've finished funding, or whether it's an income generation programme that can keep going when we're gone. To make sure that things don't fall apart – to create self-sufficiency.

I got involved in a project collecting Christmas Shoe Boxes in 1999. I got involved with that in the first year as most fellows do. The women are doing the work and they need someone to carry something. So I was asked to help out and carry stuff. The following year I helped out a bit more. I started to get a little bit more interested ... what's the issue, what's going on? The idea of the Shoe Boxes appealed to me, but who were the kids who would be receiving them? I wanted to find out. I'm nosy. I wanted to know what's going on.

The following year, I was asked if I'd take part in the volunteer team which was going to Georgia. I went and we did the meet and greet thing with all the kids. Most people on the volunteer teams want to do things ... either they are really glad they have done it and that's it, they've done their part, they can carry on with their life ... or some people go, 'I've got to do more.' Of course when I went back home two weeks later, I was going to learn how to speak Georgian and save the world. But what I did was I arranged a volunteer team to go back the following year to renovate the orphanage. I had my own business and I worked as a decorator. So that was my part. I knew how to paint. We took the team back and we spent two weeks there with the kids. At that stage, I just got hooked. I saw how it was. It's so easy to please kids. It's so easy to make them feel special. It's so easy to help.

What we basically do is relief and development. So that covers everything. Because we've only got four staff here, we work with partners. We're a Christian organisation, which means that we try to work with churches where possible. There are a lot of practical reasons for that as well as religious reasons. In general, we discovered and we feel that with Christian churches you get a couple of things: you get a correct desire to help the people. But you also get the correct desire to help the people help themselves. So teaching people to help themselves is largely what it should be about. That seems to work.

We have partners in twenty-six countries and we work with several partners within one country – for example, we have three or four partners in Romania. It's relationships and contacts that have been built over the years. In Belarus, our partner there introduced us to somebody else who is working with the deaf. So we set up a hearing programme in the mainstream school. The relationships have been building over the years. So between the four of us in the office, we have over sixty years of working in these areas.

We try to work with people who no one else is working with in general ... not always, but generally. So in other words, we try to not overlap. Overlapping is just a waste of resources. From my point of view, we try and reach as many people as possible and not overlap if other organisations are there. It's not necessarily the right or wrong approach or the right vision but it's our approach. It's just our way of doing it.

In Eastern Europe, projects tend to vary. But it tends to be different than Africa, which has its own specific level of problems. Europe tends to be more orphans and the children ... neglect tends to be a problem. It's between children

Pandi Karapanxha is a member of Beekeepers credit union in Korce, Albania, where he saved and took out a small loan to buy bee hives and start his own business. *Photo: Irish League of Credit Unions Foundation.*

and abuse and mistreatment of women. We run a lot of children's programmes in Eastern Europe … whether it's helping fund orphanages or helping with school or helping women and families recover from being badly treated either through alcohol or because of sexual abuse.

Trying to get the message across so that the public understands that the need is actually a need … it's hard sometimes. From our Shoe Box point of view, it's actually a little bit more difficult to explain without sounding too corny about it or too cute. Working on a level of progression all the time … it's more difficult to explain. For example, one of our partners in Eastern Europe wants to set up foam insulation as an income generation programme. He's seen the need. There's definitely a need on the market place. What he wants to do is use it as a rehab programme. There's a huge population of ex-narcotic users. They now need to do something to feel they are worthy. He's outlined a long-term five-year plan that, with the right funding, will actually create a self-sustaining project. Whereas if I say that we are hoping to get some money together to provide beds for an orphanage, that is much easier to sell. People would go, 'Oh, that's great.' People can relate to that much quicker. At the end of the day, if we could get the insulation project going it could generate a profit. That's a lot of what we look for – the eventual self-sustainability, not a handout all the time.

I think out of all the things that I have learned, certainly one of the most important things for me would be to set up anything so that when we leave, it keeps going … it's self-sufficient. Whether that's an education programme where people continue to go to school and get educated after we've finished funding, or whether it's an income generation programme that can keep going when we're gone. To make sure that things don't fall apart – to create self-sufficiency.

I knew a girl two years ago who emailed the office. She said she was living in West Dublin and looking to help out at the warehouse with the Shoe Boxes. So I asked her why. We had a load of emails and it came out that she was sixteen. She lived in Castleknock and she was Romanian. Her Christmas one year … herself and her sister and her mother and father lived in one room. They were very, very poor … their situation in Romania. She said that her father – despite being very poor – he tried. He put an apple and an orange out for them. That was their Christmas present. The following day or two, the local church came around and asked if they'd like to take part in the Shoe Box distribution. So she got a Shoe Box. She went from an apple and an orange to a Shoe Box that had thirty items in it. She said that she never before felt so special.

A lot of the time kids are living in vulnerable situations and they are very, very down on themselves. Kids are kids. They think they have done something wrong. The Shoe Box actually makes kids feel special … People remember. They still remember the Christmas card that was in it or the photograph with the person's name who gave the Shoe Box. Somebody made them feel special. So it does change people. It doesn't so much … it doesn't obviously set them up for life with housing and food. But a lot of what they need … what a lot of people need all over the world is self-worth and self-esteem. That's what the Shoe Boxes do. With all the kids … with the Shoe Boxes and all the kids that we help, we don't necessarily see the end result. All you see is the work in progress.

My understanding has grown over the last ten years. I started off, as most people do, with maybe a heart for helping but not with a direction to go …

my suggestion is if somebody sees a need that maybe the first step would be to go on to see what's already happening in that area or what organisations are already working in the area. Over the years, I've learned that organisations tend to get a lot more done than individuals.

I think that working with partners is the best, from our point of view, because partners who live and work in the country already know where the greatest need is and how to assess and how to approach it. How do you assess the greatest need? Local people know. If I look at this child, perhaps we can't find a home for him this time around, but his need isn't as urgent as the guy who is living on the streets … or maybe this guy who appears to be living on the street is actually living on the street only one day a week. His need isn't as great as some of the others' needs. Local partners always have local knowledge, which is ten times more effective than my knowledge. So local partners are vital. But I think it's a partnership that comes from both sides. It's important that our influence is there as well.

I think relationships are huge and important. Sitting back and listening is important … which I didn't do in the first couple of years. I sort of went in, 'This is the way I want to do it' … where now, I have learned to say or to ask, 'Is this the right way to do it?' It's changed me to a huge degree. I probably used to be a lot more selfish and self-centred for a lot of reasons. I had a family very young – I wanted more money to pay for family holidays and such – whereas now I think I've learned to think a lot more about what it's like to give. I've also learned about the benefit – which is huge. I've also learned a lot about community. The people … the relationship aspect of it .. partnership. It happens in Georgia. It happens in Ukraine, Moldova, Belarus, Armenia. It happens right across … it happens in Africa. It seems like people in these countries have nothing so they'll give you everything that they have. They respect you. They appreciate you. It doesn't matter if it's me, you, or anybody else.

'Be open to cooperation'
–Simon & Deena Walsh

Simon and Deena first became involved in Belarus in 1991 as organisers for children coming to Ireland for recuperation holidays. In 2006, they helped establish **Chernobyl Children's Trust** to help support children and families living in poverty. The organisation operates a wide range of projects in Belarus.

> **One of the things that we've learned is that you need to be more open to cooperation with other organisations, and share your information. It's certainly true the last few years, from just talking to other organisations and being open to networking, that you find out you don't know everything yourself. Yes, you might have a lot of answers to a lot of other people's queries or problems, because you've experienced it yourself, but you might find that people will reciprocate and you can benefit from their experience also.** *Simon Walsh*

Simon: We became involved as a family originally. I think it was in 1991, the first year that children were brought from Belarus to Ireland for recuperation. We met friends of ours over in Cobh and they had a couple of children with them from another country and we just asked what the story was and they said they were from Chernobyl. Chernobyl kids! And so we were just chatting about it, really, and we just said, 'How can we help, how can we get involved, what can we do?' I suppose myself and Deena have always been involved in

Children arriving into Ireland from Belarus for a recuperation holiday.
Photo: Chernobyl Children's Trust.

community organisations and helping the community one way or another so we kind of got involved that way.

A few months later we ended up on the committee in Midleton for organising holidays for kids, and we were hosting kids ourselves the following summer. We're hosting children ever since. Every year, every summer and every Christmas. Twenty-seven children we've hosted. So we just kind of got progressively more involved and probably learned as we went along. The group was set up in 2006 by volunteers that would have been experienced working in Belarus over the years and we would have had a common bond and common goal really – to work at grass roots level. We would have shared very strong knowledge of what's going on in Belarus and what is needed at a real level.

I found that there were villages and smaller towns that weren't getting aid from any organisation. There was a lot of cherry picking being done with the bigger towns that were easier to access, and you got maybe a dozen countries delivering aid to the same areas and a lot of places were being overlooked entirely. The needs are much greater in rural areas. For example, in every orphanage children have to be fed – it's a legal requirement that the children have to be fed – whereas very often we would come across children living in villages that were not being fed. I mean, we might have certain perceptions of Belarus – at this stage, believe me, it's a very well developed country in many ways – but still, go into rural areas and villages in the winter time … There's wind whistling in through the windows. It can be well into the minuses outside, sometimes temperatures can be as low as minus thirty degrees Celsius. A lot of times they might just have a sheet of plastic to keep the draught out and not much to eat inside; sometimes they mightn't be able to afford any form of heating. That's tough living.

Whereas in an orphanage the place will be warm, they'll be fed, so we tend to focus on the villages more for that reason I suppose. And about duplication again – there's very few orphanages that aren't very well looked after. Okay, the principle of orphanages is wrong and it is being phased out by government decree. Typically the problem is the government makes the decree, but won't provide resources to implement it. But at least it is a step in the right direction. So that's part of the reason, I suppose as well, that we are moving away and have moved away from orphanages, even though we have very strong links with a few specific places, and it's a bit like the humanitarian aid thing … probably being the wrong thing to do.

It would be widely accepted internationally that strategically donating humanitarian aid to any country is the wrong thing to do in the long term, in that it creates a culture of dependency. But, you go into a village and you see the needs, do you wait for the long-term solution to come along or do you fulfil the needs if you can, even in the short term? And ok sure what you need to do, is do both in tandem … our take on humanitarian aid is that we will try to fill needs where we can while trying to effect longer term solutions if possible by working with local organisations and administrations. Of course, it's about a process of education as well as putting structures in place.

Sometimes it can be very complex trying to support families as well. I know again that strategically, in the long term, that direct support isn't probably always the right thing to do, but sometimes there are certain needs to be met. You have to be very careful about families, if there's an alcohol problem for example. So sometimes you have to help indirectly, like for example, children that might not be getting fed at all, and if you provide food for them, the food will be sold for alcohol or other things. So we might do things like pay some money to the local school to give them dinner. Maybe an extra meal or something. We've done that, quite a bit. So, you know, sometimes you have to be a bit creative in how you do things.

It can be very difficult going into particularly poor situations, and it can be the embarrassment factor of the family, with an outsider coming in. What we've kind of found over the years is that you need to keep going back and build a bit of trust. We always tend to try and keep people's dignity to the fore, and just treat people with respect really, I suppose. Like when you're going into somebody's situation, a family that are trying really hard, they just don't have the resources to get beyond a certain level and they never will. You just have to be very careful how you help that family, in a dignified way. It's about allowing them to accept you, and it's how to deal with that, in a human and dignified way, which you need to keep sight of at all times. It tends to work really well, they tend to understand that we're being very respectful, and we're not treating them as anything less than ourselves. And that's very important.

We don't go looking for families to help. They'll be brought to our attention by a local organisation for example that would know about what we're doing, but that local organisation may not be able to give any help. And that's often how we're brought into the equation. Sometimes it'll happen by chance, if we're visiting a village for some other purpose, and we might meet somebody, or see a situation, and then try and see what can be done. It is very delicate, and sometimes you know, you go in, because there's a house and it's really, really poor – and they don't want any help. And that's fine as well.

I suppose a lot of the people who went out to Romania, or Belarus, volunteers working for families, might not necessarily have the qualifications to know about a lot of the things. I would have put myself in that category. There's a lot of learning involved in that. We're still learning. But again, we would be lucky in that we had good local advice as well. And typically the organisations that would partner with us in the community would have a lot of professional people working. So we would take their advice, and discuss what is the best plan of action for a family or for an area.

We tend to explain, as well, how we operate and how we get our funds. Like initially people over there thought we just spent money and everybody in the West is loaded; whereas now they mostly understand that we're just ordinary people, ordinary families, and we have to work really hard to generate funds and we don't pick it up off the streets. We actually work hard to come up with individual ways of raising funds and I think when they understand that it gives them a different perspective.

Deena: We are tied in with a lovely programme in Gomel in southern Belarus. We are involved with thirty or so families, who have children with varying disabilities and are, unusually for Belarus, living at home ... different disabilities and their needs are different too. We have supported them with practical things like specialised medical equipment, wheelchairs and aid and by helping with taking the kids on holidays once a year in holiday camps within Belarus. A lot of it is about spoiling their mothers a little and giving them some respite and a bit of quality of life, because they've had zero, really. We're talking about profoundly disabled kids and sometimes terminally ill kids and mothers looking after them 24/7 at home.

I suppose it's about confidence building, really. I always see our organisation as a kind of back up support rather than the one that is changing the world as such. I mean, yes, they wouldn't probably have a wheelchair-adapted minivan if we didn't provide it, or they mightn't have a lot of equipment if we didn't provide it, that kind of thing. But whereas before each of these families were alone, now they have developed to a high degree from just interacting with one another, and I suppose we maybe have just been the catalyst. Maybe we just gave them the confidence to do more for themselves ... now they're becoming a lot more proactive themselves and coming up with new ideas. And they say no to us sometimes, which is not bad either. Victoria's the one who runs the organisation. I came up with what I thought was a brilliant idea recently, and she had confidence enough to say, 'I'm sorry, but that's not going to work.' So in one way it was great to hear that, because, you know, three years ago she wouldn't have said that to me.

Simon: What's starting to happen in Belarus that's new is that some organisations that we are working with, if there is any industry or successful company in the area, they will try and tap into them for some sponsorship or funding to pay for the children's holidays, or to buy something. Just to put a bit of responsibility back on the Belarusian companies as well. And that's kind of a new thing, I think that was part of the confidence building thing as well – you know, confidence to ask for help locally – 'You get companies to give you money? Maybe we could try that here.' So yeah, I mean, like we're only there as back up, really. I mean, we'll never change the world. They will have to change that, themselves.

I've one abiding memory of arriving with humanitarian aid maybe in the late '90s to an orphanage in the south of Belarus. And we were in a queue behind, I think, four organisations, and that's when I said, 'There's something wrong with this equation', and we found out that the queue was a queue of trucks delivering aid to the same orphanage, so I was surprised to find that there was huge duplication going on, and still is to a certain extent.

One of the things that we've learned is that you need to be more open to cooperation with other organisations, and share your information. It's certainly true the last few years, from just talking to other organisations and being open to networking, that you find out you don't know everything yourself. Yes, you might have a lot of answers to a lot of other people's queries or problems, because you've experienced it yourself, but you might find that people will reciprocate and you can benefit from their experience also.

And it's purely through networking with other organisations that you can be a lot more effective. Organisations can save money, save resources, save time. Tiny example: we were making an aid delivery to a community organisation in a town in Belarus, and just through talking to another Irish organisation, we discovered they were about to do a building project in the same town. They were trying to get building materials out to the town, but they had no way of getting it out there. So we happened to be going to the town, had a bit of spare room in the truck, or created it, ran out their materials for them, saved them all the hassle of getting out there, and the cost, and they subsequently could do a little something else for us, so that's a small example. And if you applied that globally you could get organisations working a lot more smartly.

Another example: there is this highly intelligent young woman of twenty-two, she is wheelchair bound, and we have tried to help her get a college place, or employment. But it's always like knocking on a closed door. We actually managed to get her a job at one stage, but she would have had to find her own way from where she was living to the place of employment, and because she's in a wheelchair, it's not possible. Because you can't get on public transport in Belarus if you're in a wheelchair, no taxi driver will take you. So opportunities are just closed, if you are disabled. It'll take a lot more than one organisation before anyone can solve those kinds of problems.

Certainly employment initiatives, developing rural communities and creating acceptance of disabilities, that's a big, big undertaking and no one organisation is going to do it. Sure, one organisation can chip away and try and change things, put in a few structures into one or two villages, or orphanages and try and get it replicated elsewhere, but to take it globally, on a countrywide basis, you're going to need a lot of countries working together, a lot of organisations working together.

'Treat everyone as an individual'
–Audrey Cranston

Audrey (34) first travelled to Romania in 2000 with **Health Action Overseas** as a volunteer in Negru Voda orphanage for children with disabilities. She spent a year in Romania and went on to become the CEO of Health Action Overseas, overseeing its work in Romania and China.

> **The whole disability approach that's current and up to date is about individuals. It's about treating everybody as an individual, and having dignity and respect for what they want to do. So it's like, I'll do what I want with my life, you do what you want with your life. And previous to this, we've all been telling these people with disability what to do with their lives, we've been telling them they should live in a group home, or they should live here, or live there. But the approach that we've come more to adopt is more about, 'what do you want to do?'**

When I first went, I was there for a year and a month, thirteen months. Negru Voda is in the back of beyond, so horse and cart, about an hour's drive from Constanta, and the institution was the main money spinner in the village. There was a flour-making factory as well, so there were basically only two jobs you could have: you can either work in the orphanage, or work in the flour mill.

Health Action Overseas had, for the ten years previous to that, been using volunteers, so they had been going out in their droves to work in the institution,

Two residents of a group home in Constanta, Romania, who formerly lived in institutional care. *Photo: Health Action Overseas.*

in a caring capacity. And the year or two before I went over, they had pulled all volunteers out. There was a very defined change in the need identified. Before it was about keeping people alive, and the volunteers were necessary when you needed extra hands, and to feed and to clean, and to stimulate and play, and they brought a lot of love with them. So that went on for ten years as well as trucks of aid, it may have been hundreds of trucks of aid going over, but that all stopped in the year prior to me going over. And there already was a development team in place, rather than what we call volunteering.

I think that there were over 200 children there at that time. And they'd just crowd people together in corridors and rooms, just mass management. They'd just herd, just herded like animals really. And when you'd arrive, you'd always be the centre of attention, you know, it was great excitement for somebody to come. I just remember it was an assault on the senses, it was just really intimidating,

We employed – I'd say we had ten people in the therapy centre, ten local people. We set up the programmes then, and the aim was to try and have everybody to have a treatment or an activity, a group activity. So it was really, really, really interesting stuff. I had never any interest or experience in the field of therapy or education or anything like that before, and you know, now I'm hugely interested in it, and I've started doing my degree in disability. I was twenty-three at the time with very limited experience, and going into an unknown environment. You could easily look back and say, with hindsight, that it was incredibly foolish. I was the luckiest person, because I got the experience. It was a huge experience.

At first, the staff who were working in the institution, I thought they were lazy, I thought they were cold, I thought they were indifferent. Because they've got all these kids, and they were barely kept clean, and they were barely fed – there was no get up and go, or enthusiasm. You didn't see much love or affection, so my initial thinking was, 'Oh my God who are these people?' I think there's still a lot of indifference around. If you went to the institutions, there's a huge amount of indifference, but I think I've come to understand better why it's there.

You know, it's hard to work with someone who stinks, or that has faeces on them, or who has put their hands down into their nappy and now has hands covered in it. That's a hard ask of anybody, of any human being. And to get paid bad money for it, and not have the right resources, and not have hot water to wash them, and not have enough staff to do all the rounds. You can look at the picture and you can understand totally why anybody would be de-motivated, and not want to do the extra little bit. But then, in saying that, I have to say that I did meet some of the most amazing people, that were working really diligently, and effectively, without any kind of training, just some people that were naturals, that came from the heart. And it just made a huge difference in people's lives. Absolutely huge difference.

So HAO opened the first group home in 2001 with adults from the institution. The idea then was that group homes were the way forward. People who moved into a group home, albeit they all had a mild disability, no one thought that they'd ever, ever move beyond the group home. But then it became very obvious with the work that had been done with them, that they were incredibly capable. They've ended up with jobs, and it became increasingly obvious that they wanted to have relationships, and possibly get married, and that they were capable of more independence. So then we opened two independent living apartments.

The whole disability approach that's current and up to date is about individuals. It's about treating everybody as an individual, and having dignity and respect for what they want to do. So it's like, I'll do what I want with my life, you do what you want with your life. And previous to this, we've all been telling these people with disability what to do with their lives, we've been telling them they should live in a group home, or they should live here, or live there. But the approach that we've come more to adopt is more about, 'what do you want to do?'

It's only a very small minority of people that we're dealing with who actually can't tell you what they want to do in some shape or fashion. Or what their interests are. And it's not just about where they want to live, or do they want to live on their own or with a boyfriend or a girlfriend; it's about what they want to spend their time doing, because a lot of people just assume that they want to paint pictures, or do art, you know? Some people want to dye their hair pink, or blue, or green, or start listening to rock music.

And you start to build the person. It's not just about feeding – it is initially, about feeding and putting a roof over their head, their medical needs, but then, once those are met, it has to be more, because it can't stop there. It doesn't stop there for any of us. They're equal human beings, so it's about them identifying and working, and giving them experiences in life, to find out what they want to do. What it is that makes them happy. And what their possibilities are.

It's not perfect, it's a work in progress, all the time. When everybody is in a job, people slap themselves on the back and say, 'Aren't we great, we've got everybody employed.' But it's the first job some of them have had. Some of them are pushing trolleys down at the Metro, some are washing cars. Hello? What's their next job? They're going to get bored. And that's what we're hearing already, people start getting bored with the job. They should be able to earn more money, or do something a little bit more challenging. I've changed my job ten times, they should have every right to change their job ten times. So it's very much about support there.

We look after people and we think we're great, but by doing everything for these people we're taking away their sense of value and their sense of esteem. So it's about letting them do something for themselves, that they want to do. Where they can earn their value, and feel their value. And feel like they are a valuable member of society, get to know the neighbours. And provide opportunities for them to get to know the neighbours, and their names, and chat and stuff like that.

Even if they are in institutional care you can still work at that – institutions will never be the answer, and they never provide what's needed for people adequately. There'll never be an equal citizen living in an institution. Never. That doesn't mean that they should be just left there to fester until such time that somebody does something. There's still things that can be done. But it's not the answer. It isn't the answer.

There's still people in Ireland learning. There's still institutions in Ireland, loads of organisations that aren't doing it right in Ireland, that are providing care, and telling people what to do, and telling people what they're having for dinner. F*** off. Let people tell you what they want for dinner. But it's up to the Romanian people to get to grips with the problem, and the Romanian people to fight the cause. Because there's no point in me fighting it, and I grasped this late as well, there's no point in me going to Romania and standing in administration offices, and fighting in their corner. I'm gone. We're all gone, at some point. And the people who are left behind, if they're not up to speed, then all we've done is lost, if they can't carry it on. Or else we're going to be there forever, doing the bits and pieces, which is not sustainable.

'Do more with the money'
–Henry Deane

Henry (62) has worked in Roscrea as an auctioneer and civil servant for over thirty years. He set up **Chernobyl Lifeline** in 1991 to bring children affected by the Chernobyl disaster to Ireland for rest and recuperation holidays.

> I'm less inclined to bring in children to Ireland now, because you do have the situation where they go back unhappy, you know, to their own humble home having left relative luxury in Ireland. Back then it was less difficult to organise the paperwork, it was less difficult to organise the funds. I think, you know, rather than bring the children here, that if we give the money over there, we can do more with the money. Our money will go further.

Almost twenty years ago a friend of mine was inside a shop in Roscrea and when she came out … two little children ran across to the car to see who could get the front seat and one was a Chernobyl kid and the other was the family child. I was so taken by this and so impressed by the Chernobyl child and the Irish child coming together that I immediately talked to my wife about it, I was so smitten with the idea.

The first child we took in was a little girl called Natasha. The Iron Curtain had just come down, so getting calls in and out was almost impossible, but we communicated with her again and again and within twelve months I was heading up an organisation and we gave it the name Chernobyl Lifeline and that's how it began. Since 1991, into our house, there was a minimum of two children every summer, and sometimes up to five. We would bring them in June and they would have stayed until the end of August. Yep, we would take them for the entire summer holidays. We used to always bring over young teenagers, because my daughter was a teenager at the time and that was the idea for each group. We built up a fantastic rapport with them.

The group were bringing in an average of forty children per month for June, July, August and December every year. We always had the Christmas group. Things are changing, though, and we don't bring as many children now. In the beginning we all felt, rightly or wrongly, that to give them – for even a month or six weeks – give them good uncontaminated air, good clean food and all that, and send them back happy and comfortable and well dressed, that you would have cleaned out their systems to a real extent from the contamination. I was one of the first ever to organise repeat visits back in the early 1990s and it was frowned upon. People said, 'Look there's so many children; we should only bring them once.' But we said to the families, 'If you want the child brought back, you give the money for the ticket and we will organise everything.' And we did. It was only a direct flight so it was reasonable, so the children would come back over and over again.

We brought children from villages, because we felt that at least the children in the orphanages were being taken care of. Not very well, but they were being housed and looked after. We found ourselves mostly dealing with children from broken homes … in a relationship where one of the parents was alcoholic, or one of the parents was out of work, or marriage breakup, single parents …

I do think little villages out from the big cities – some are still falling through the net. I think mainly because of a tremendous sense of hopelessness … the alcoholism is a serious problem. In Ireland we call it poteen, in America moonshine, in Belarus it's *samogon* – they make this stuff themselves and they just destroy themselves with it. But it's a long, slow suicide brought about by just hopelessness, and there are children who are suffering because their parents' relationships are breaking up, because they're turning to alcohol.

You can help right down on the ground. Right down on the ground. Because I'm always afraid that by going in and working and doing up a hospital, that you're really saving the government cost, that the government can rub their hands and say, 'Well, the hospital is going to be renewed by an Irish group', you know what I mean? But children on the ground, and I was always very affected by that, when you go over and go into the little country schools

Residents with staff and volunteers in the Community Room of an Independent Living Project for young adults with disabilities in Belarus. *Photo: Chernobyl Children International.*

and go in there, and you see teachers who are trying very hard, but hopelessness again, they don't have the funds. And I think they would … I do know there's corruption … but you have to get past that and find someone you can trust who will deal with a child who shows a little promise.

There were children that came to my home that are now adults and teachers and some of them have difficulties with the children in their classes with their mobile phones. So there, Belarus has come a long way. But the times when we used to bring children over … Probably the thing that struck me the most was that it was so easy to impress these children; that the smallest thing was a big thing to them – like a full fridge, bananas, apples, these were luxuries to these children at that time; but life has changed.

There's dozens of organisations in Ireland, and they've all been bringing children from Belarus to Ireland for years. Thousands and thousands down through the past twenty years coming, all these children. There's great camaraderie there, but it's only on the family level, it never went up to the political level. The Belarusian government tried on a number of occasions to stop children coming to Ireland and there was a big outcry. I think the government saw it as a contamination … children coming to Ireland and seeing how we lived and going back and being fed up with their own situation.

When you would meet ordinary people and you broke down the barriers, then you would have friends for life. The ordinary individual whose children came to Ireland, my God, the guilt we would feel walking into their tiny little apartment, them putting on a massive spread for us of every kind of food … You know, they put on the effort, they loved us coming and they felt very bad if we went to another child's house and not to their house, so you would spend most of your time just socialising and going to their houses rather than spending your time working, but I suppose it was important. It was important to them.

Some of the people we met felt that the Irish government paid us for working there. Nothing we could do or say would convince them otherwise. They believed the Irish government was funding our efforts and it took away this understanding and this appreciation of what we were doing. How could you when they looked upon it as being just a job of work that we were doing for them? You couldn't educate them to the fact that we were standing in the snow outside the church gates collecting the pennies and tuppences to fund our efforts and we were putting in the effort and doing it ourselves.

I'm less inclined to bring in children to Ireland now, because you do have the situation where they go back unhappy, you know, to their own humble home having left relative luxury in Ireland. Back then it was less difficult to organise the paperwork, it was less difficult to organise the funds. I think, you know, rather than bring the children here, that if we give the money over there, we can do more with the money. Our money will go further. It was less difficult in the past, because there were direct flights. There are difficulties now with the government in Belarus and also our own government bringing in very stringent regulations. The paperwork is a lot for people who are volunteering and we never had a lot of people involved in our committee.

So we are now in the process of moving more to Ukraine. We feel that Ukraine is in more need for a number of reasons, but the main reason is that in Belarus now, a lot of the orphanages and schools are well cared for, and that some number of groups in Ireland are dealing with each little facility in Belarus. That's not the situation in Ukraine, particularly when you go down south into Ukraine, it's severe poverty and we feel that in the villages and towns there are little groups of people who are trying to help themselves. In

Ukraine they are willing to try, so we feel that we should try and help them. We're hoping also that those children in need of a holiday, we'll give them a holiday, but not here. In the Ukraine there's one of the finest holiday resorts in the world down at the Black Sea – Odessa. Magnificent. Now the cost will be a tiny percentage of what it would be to bring them to Ireland and I feel the children would benefit more.

Having said that, there's children who came to us who now have grown up and have married and some are living in Ireland, and I've kept in touch with each of them. I keep in touch with a lot of them, most of them are no longer children, they're now in their late twenties and married with children of their own. So getting their feedback and the continued feedback down through the years it leaves me no doubt that giving the children a holiday here was good for them.

It was part of our life in Roscrea for a long time. A member of our group was saying the thing he misses the most is the big groups of children; all the families on a Saturday and a Sunday coming to Mass, coming to shopping, and you'd see all the little Chernobyl children and you'd meet them. He misses that a lot. So if there isn't going to be as high a profile with seeing the children here and coaches coming in from Shannon bringing in all these children and getting down off the coach and the photographs in the local papers, you can't replicate that. There is a great benefit of having the children here in the shops and going round the streets and that. There was a presence and it was easier to raise funds because of that. I see the African charities now, they send us photographs of the children we've adopted and are putting through school so you have a little letter from the child and you have the child's picture and you can relate to that.

We won't walk away from Belarus, because there is that link there with the entire town of Mikashevichi, in Brest region; we have a commitment to that and we're not going to walk away from it. I've enjoyed every moment of it, every moment of it, it's been one of the great blessings of my life. We have been in a very lucky, very good situation where we could share all we have with the kids in Belarus, and thanks be to God that it continues. I hope it continues.

'Persuade the decision makers'
–John Mulligan

John (59) became involved in managing construction projects with Trade Aid in 1992, in Romania and Russia. He helped found **Focus on Romania** in 1999, primarily to highlight the problems in state services for people with disabilities in Romania and to lobby for reform.

> I've spent more time over the last ten years sitting down with politicians, trying to get them round to my point of view. If you get a Minister just thinking, you're away. But unless you persuade the decision makers ... bottom up, you're only making tiny dents in it, and a top-down decision can undo everything you've done in a minute. But use anything you do, any contact you have to get your feet under the table of influence, and to get around the table where decisions are made.

I was always very, very interested in Eastern Europe, and the whole issue of the divided Europe. I remember as soon as the Berlin wall fell, I was in Brussels on some business, and I drove to Prague, which was a nine-hour drive. I queued up and got across the border very shortly after they opened up. One of my most vivid memories of it, apart from the rusting farm equipment and decaying infrastructure, is of seeing a brightly lit shop window and a crowd of people outside it, and I walked down the street and joined the crowd looking in the window and saw a pyramid of Pedigree Chum tins. There was the culture and everything else, but that was my abiding memory of Prague at that moment.

Mass grave for children who died at Negru Voda orphanage in Constanta, Romania. *Photo: John Mulligan/ Focus on Romania.*

Trade Aid was an initiative by trades instructors, to provide assistance to NGOs who were bogged down in Romania with bad infrastructure and problems. I was asked to get involved in an assessment. I took the week off, got the credit card, and booked a flight and went to Bucharest. In Bucharest at that time, there were no cars in the city, very few cars, just trucks and buses, grass growing up through the street. It was like India, people sitting on the railway tracks, you know, everyone was travelling by train, because there was no other way to go around.

In the following years we went to an orphanage down south near Constanta; I was fully on board at this stage, and it was becoming a bit of a permanent occupation. It was hard to get materials at that time, so we trucked the materials over. But we took a view also that we would do everything to Romanian standards – there was no argument about that – particularly electrical, plumbing, things like that; we thought you have to adhere to those, because the wiring systems are the polar opposite of the way they're done in Western Europe. I was lucky I was dropped into an organisation that treated every job as a construction contract. They sent a scout over a couple of weeks beforehand evaluating the job, they made a programme of what was to be done, there was no deviation unless we had time at the end.

When we got started at first – it was a bit like the war would be over at Christmas, we thought this was a temporary measure until Romania got onto its feet. It was kind of a solidarity with Romanian people who had been colonised, and I think that was in common with a lot of NGOs. We thought they'd start to build their own structures and start sorting out their own problems. We found out that not only was that not the case, but they were – there was a whole industry around the theft of aid, for instance.

Initially I never questioned the need for people to be in institutions, didn't question that at all. Didn't question why these people were here. The issue to me was one of their accommodation being bad and not up to standard, and this was an emergency situation brought around by years of decline of infrastructure. And to some extent, that was the case. But the underlying thing, as to why the people were there in the first place, hadn't occurred to me at that point. Later I began to understand that people with disabilities were hidden away – to present a face to the world that we don't have second class citizens, we don't have second rate human beings, people with disabilities – and there was a tacit understanding that they wouldn't live long and that was a self-fulfilling prophecy.

For the first few years we accepted it – that disabled people are kept in institutions in these conditions, and it's just that. But we began thinking about the bigger picture, about closing the places down; we began to ask these kinds of questions. It was a gradual realisation of a lot of things. We saw the difference in the appearance and the demeanour of six kids who were in a group home, as distinct from the 300 that were across the fence in the institution. It was so different, the behaviour, everything was different. I saw them sitting down at tables and having dinner together and interacting like kids would in a family, and choosing what to have on TV, making a choice, things like that. We were at a disadvantage in not coming from the care background. Maybe we would have understood all of this at an earlier stage.

So we set up Focus on Romania primarily as a lobby group, to bring this to the attention of the European Union, because Romania was an applicant country and they were a long way down the accession road at this point. We saw an opportunity with the application process to put pressure on them to reform their disabilities sector. Our stated aim was to focus world attention on the problem of inadequate state care of children and young adults in institutions in Romania.

Initially our aim was to close Negru Voda orphanage. We didn't look at a national picture. We thought if we can get these 300 youngsters into some kind of decent life, get them out of there – because the conditions were diabolical. They were diabolical. And we started to lobby, and we started to get noticed. We made a film with RTE of Negru Voda. It created a most almighty row, politically; there was uproar. It resulted in the Minister being sacked, the director being sacked. They sacked people all the way up the line to Bucharest. We'd also been battering the European Union with the One Million Emails campaign. We had been really cranking up the political pressure, in a big way. Every chance we got, we cranked it up. And when the Romanian government came here on their pre-accession tour of Europe, we gave them a hell of a hard time.

The most active part of that operation was in the years prior to Romania joining the EU. In 2005, 2006, it was very busy for us, because we were going to Romania every couple of months to meet with the local authority, or the department, the national authority for disability, to drag along the project, to make the project happen. And to make it happen, to keep the wheels spinning, we were putting pressure on in Brussels as well. And every time we came up against a lull in the project, we were back to Brussels, and created a stink there. It was a once-off moment in time to lobby, strongly. We were trying to stop, ostensibly, Romania joining the EU. That was the front end of what we were doing.

Eventually the orphanage was closed and we got funding for a new pilot centre for the young people. We also got a commitment that they would set up a department within the national authority for persons with disability, which was the government sub department dealing with it, that they would set up a department or a unit to create policies and standards.

In Romania, people are afraid of their politicians, and they're quite often afraid to stand up. Our problems in Ireland are entirely down to corruption – I'm not talking about just being handed a bag of cash to just do something with, it's about not making decisions in the common good, in the interest of the common good. Making decisions for a sectional interest group who should not be given any kind of advantage. So corruption is the root cause. As indeed, most of the problems in Ireland are corruption. I suppose as long as people keep electing corrupt politicians, no more than here, the problems won't be resolved. Not everybody wants to put themselves in the firing line for constant flak from governments and things like that. It's not a comfortable place to be.

I've spent more time over the last ten years sitting down with politicians, trying to get them round to my point of view. If you get a Minister just thinking, you're away. But unless you persuade the decision makers … bottom up, you're only making tiny dents in it, and a top-down decision can undo everything you've done in a minute. But use anything you do, any contact you have to get your feet under the table of influence, and to get round the table where decisions are made.

But the slog of making progress is very – it's dull and not very exciting and it's very unrewarding sometimes. It's just a hard slog to make progress, very slow and piecemeal, doing it little by little. But at the end of the day, the rewards in it are – for example, I go down to Constanta occasionally to visit some of the lads who are now living in the community, and I go and sit down at the table, and we have our dinner together, and they're all up to me, showing me their homework and their stuff, and that's a reward, you couldn't buy that.

It should be like that for everybody, everybody's entitled to that, you know. It's a basic human right, and because you have a bad leg or something, it doesn't mean you should be in this screaming hellhole of a place. So, every victory is a victory, but then you look at the bigger picture and it's like a big black cloud. You know, between all the organisations over the last twenty years, we've got maybe a couple of hundred people into a better life, but there's still thousands and thousands we haven't. And when you look at the better ones, it's cheering, but when you look back behind you at what you haven't done … it can be depressing at times and you can think … I haven't succeeded here.

But I suppose we've done a little bit, we're part of what happened and nobody is unaware now that there is a problem, an ongoing problem in Romania. There are different methodologies, you don't have to go in and kick the door in. I go in and bang the table, literally, and say what the f*** are you doing here? And other people I know will go in and establish relationships with people and then say, 'Look, would it not be better to do it this way? And we can show you how, and we can help you.' In a quiet way I've seen that that's very persuasive.

When we started there was a particular state of collapse of society and the emergency response was a good response at that point; we kept people alive that would have died. A lot of people would have died, and we kept them alive by – even simple things, like getting the heating to work, getting the water clean, putting in sanitation, allowing them to cook food to proper temperature. Things like that. Basic emergency stuff. You could still go back to Romania and do that, every day. You could put thousands of volunteers back in Romania and they'd have a lifetime of work doing just that.

I suppose we were naive in some ways, in that we felt sorry for the kids in the institution, we thought their life was not good, and we wanted to improve it. We didn't have any interest in being permanent aid workers, you know. The last thing that I want to be doing in the middle of winter in Brussels is to fight a case with the European Commission. We've no interest in any of this, really, we just want it fixed, and get on with it. And it is so easy to fix, the cost of keeping people in the community is much the same as keeping them in the institutions.

We were never in this for the kudos, we went in to solve a problem. Quite often egos get in the way of progress, because people don't want their idea to be taken on by somebody else, and they're secretive about it. I don't care, I just want an end to the suffering really, and I don't care who does it.

'It's all about trust'

–Stephen Wilson

Stephen (30) has been involved in aid work in the Balkans through the Adventist Church from an early age and lived in Albania from 2001 to 2003. He now works as a minister and with **Adventist Development and Relief Agency**, supporting community development in eight countries, including Albania, where the focus is on building clinics and schools in rural areas.

> Choosing a village to work in is the hardest thing. For example, if we had forty grand to rebuild a school, and every village has a school, which village do you choose to build it in – the one that has the worst school or the best teachers? We always went for the best teachers and it worked out okay. Basically, if you knew someone there then you had more trust ... that's how we chose it.

How I first went ... I knew a guy teaching English in Albania, so I just went down to visit for a couple of weeks. I remember being shocked by the fact that it was a Muslim country. It never even dawned on me there would be a Muslim country in Europe. I guess it's from that visit I got more involved ... I lived in Albania from 2001 to 2003, so that's when the more in-depth work happened.

Officially I was a missionary, but most of the work I was doing was related to teaching English language. We were building a centre while we were there as well ... basically for women, because it was quite a male-dominated society ... we built quite a nice centre so the women and kids could have a place to meet. Then in villages around we would do health campaigns and go and teach them to brush their teeth or do a week's English language course. We got involved with some Italian groups that were rebuilding village clinics, so I was helping around with that. Basically everything ... it was kind of hard to separate the faith side of it from the social side of it early on. But when we started to work in the villages it became more focused on the development side, especially teaching programmes about health. I remember we got deeply involved with the people at that stage.

I guess in the beginning the work was maybe too friendship-based, it didn't have any structure or purpose. We were great fun, and people will remember when the Irish came, but they might not have learned too much. If you give people a structure and an idea, they can do a lot more for themselves.

The shocking thing you notice when you go to see these isolated villages is that they have no school, no clinic, no social place to meet. After communism fell there was no place for communities to meet and there's no longer trust among them. Everyone was leaving their villages – old people and young kids left – and it wasn't very sustainable. So in the beginning the focus was hygiene and English language clubs, but it changed over the years. When the Kosovo crisis ended, ADRA focused on community clinics and schools as the two important public buildings that might encourage people to stay. That was pretty much the basis of the work: every village should have a good school and a good clinic, so they know if they get sick or have kids, they have some reason to stay there.

Every culture has some system to care for their kids, to ensure the poor are looked after, but most of the 'official development' in Albania I'm aware of has nothing to do with primary level education or healthcare. There are a lot of investments that are happening in big things, yet there's little investment in primary education or health from the state. If you have high blood pressure and you need to take tablets, there's no support for that. There's no money to renovate the school or provide desks. Yet these are the things that people worry about, and talk about most often, but these are the things that are forgotten.

The majority of primary schools are not near the standard they need to be. The university in Tirana is fabulous with lovely new buildings, and government offices are beautiful; but if you go to an isolated village, the plaster is falling through the roof of the school, the windows are single pane, the building has a mud roof and there are holes in the desks. Kids still have

Part of an Irish volunteer team helping to renovate the school and nurses' station in Kloc, Southern Albania in 2008. *Photo: Adventist Development and Relief Agency.*

to bring wood for the fire. It all feels so wrong. The kids don't bother going to school. Parents say kids are more likely to get sick in school and they feel they can provide better for the kids at home. But even still, in the most remote villages, parents know that education is important.

My personal understanding of development is removing the obstacles to people having a full and happy life. The reality is that a lot of those barriers are out of my control. I'd love to change a tax system, but I can't. But the areas where you can be most helpful are health and education … you can actually get involved with them.

A village elder may be the official one responsible, but the nurses are the ones that are at the coalface, so you can understand a lot through them. That's why I think road building and electrification and all these bigger projects are not really development. You're developing something, but not necessarily helping the people. But if they're healthy and have a good education, they can fight for their own land or invest in their own things. For example, one thing that really surprised me this year was that in the village, almost everyone had a greenhouse. They were big greenhouses – up to an acre. The husband would work six months a year in Greece to be able send money home to build the greenhouse. Now they have somewhere to plant tomatoes and sell them – so why would I give money or grants for that when people can do it themselves?

When I first went, it felt like people were begging. Yeah ... too nice to you and saying, 'Well, if you can fix this school why not fix the next one in the next village?' It was a bit difficult, but I think things have changed. Back then they didn't know what investment meant. It was a bit of a mad rush ... Now every sign on the road says, 'This money has been invested by the World Bank' or the EU or whatever and this is how much it costs and when it'll finish. So people have come to understand something is built because of money and it comes from somewhere so they have much more respect for the donor.

It is important for the community to see the buildings that are built as their own. The building we renovated three years ago had previously been renovated with UN funding and basically the people in the village didn't take care about it or see it as their own. Within three years the school ended up in worse condition than before, because it wasn't cared for or maintained. But after we did it up, things were a bit different. We went back two years after we finished building it and it was well maintained and no donkeys are walking through it. It's the kind of thing people have pride in. I think it's because we were volunteers and we built up friendships with the people, and also the quality of work.

Choosing a village to work in is the hardest thing. For example, if we had forty grand to rebuild a school, and every village has a school, which village do you choose to build it in – the one that has the worst school or the best teachers? We always went for the best teachers and it worked out okay. Basically, if you knew someone there then you had more trust ... that's how we chose it.

If you work through the elders, or if people have seen you in the past, they know a little more about you and trust you. It's all about trust, and the fact that your gear doesn't get stolen, that's pure trust. So if you do it officially through the elders it's easier. This year we had a photographer going around taking pictures of life in the village and we had told the elder and nurse what we were going to do. They spread the word around and so when we went around with the camera, people weren't as embarrassed. They knew exactly what we were doing and it made that project so much easier. I was surprised at how much people opened up and told more of their story than they would have normally.

We now have to present any training material to the village elders in advance so they know what we're going to talk about. They're always nervous we're going to moralise or preach, which was a bit difficult this year, because one of our campaigns was about violence against women. It was a bit scary out in the village talking about that with a group of men, telling them that they should give women their own money so they can make their own choices and that your community will be better if women feel more freedom. But the worst thing would be to ignore these issues, skim over them – you have to talk about these issues as well. The elders were a little bit nervous, but I think the fact that we told them everything we were going to say built up a lot of trust.

You get Albanian volunteers coming to help us in their final year of high school and when you're chatting with them about colleges, you realise it's so easy to be a negative cultural impact. There's still this idea that if something comes from the West, it's better. But most of the things you get from abroad are more processed, more expensive and generally not as good. Volunteers must learn from the people and respect them. Ten years ago the focus was on teaching people about hygiene, but that's gone and now it's replaced with cultural learning and sharing. That is probably more important than the training and teaching kids English that we did in the past.

You can get something across better working on the site or chatting in the café than in a seminar. If you preach a sermon on the weekend, people won't pay any attention to you. But if you visit them in their homes during the week and discuss the same subject, that's when you really start to see some changes. It is hard, because you don't always have all the answers and you have to listen. I mean, their attitudes towards family and respect for family is great, but their attitude to women and respect for women is different. That's why I think the culture part really goes hand-in-hand with development.

'Invest in the local economy'
–Michael Kinsella

Michael (58) is an electrician from Wicklow and first travelled to Moldova in 2001 where he was involved in construction at an orphanage. He subsequently set up **Ierlande Moldova** in 2006 to work in a residential institution for adults with disabilities and psychiatric problems in Badiceni village, near Soroca in the north of Moldova. He has also been involved with renovation projects in Belarus.

> What's the best way to help? If you could – employment. If you could, employ local people. It's the answer if you can employ local people, because you put money into the economy. If you've got the money or you have the wherewithal to get the money, it's much better to buy what you want in Moldova and employ Moldovan people to do it. That's better for Moldova.

I went to work in Moldova in an orphanage in 2001 with some other volunteers. We got to know people who worked there, we got to know the children who lived there, and we became interested in what happened to them after they turned eighteen. There was a thing that children who misbehaved were warned that if you misbehave, you'll be sent to Soroca. So where is it? Nobody knew, nobody could tell us. So then we would enquire as to what would happen to the girls when they got older – eighteen, twenty, whatever – to find out that they go to different institutions in Balti and Soroca. But Soroca was the one that was feared by everyone and I didn't know why.

We as Irish people felt we were doing things good for the children at the orphanage … children are only children until they're eighteen, and for the next sixty or seventy years they're going to be adults, who's going to look for these people then? So I went back, and looked at different institutions in the north, a few different places I went to, and I made four attempts to get into Soroca, and on three occasions I wasn't let in, and on the fourth occasion the director wasn't there and I was let in.

I was overawed with the size of the place. I was overawed with the fact that it was rundown, there was absolutely no sanitary conditions of any kind, other than a tap and a garden hose in some of the toilets, not all of them, and the place was falling down. It was the wintertime when I went there, it was probably the end of October I think, and people were dragged through the muck and through the snow, people who couldn't walk were dragged inside, they were fed in buckets like dogs. They had very poor clothing, they had no winter clothing, they were huddled up like rats together for the warmth. It was a horrible place, there was a horrible smell in it, there were extremely physically sick people there, the food was slop and the people had no quality of life.

So I came back to Ireland and I set up our organisation, which enabled us to gather volunteers, and I'm an electrician so the first thing I had to do was to buy tools for people to work with. We sent the tools over to Moldova and we brought volunteers of all walks of life, trades people and medical people and ordinary people who are more valuable in actual fact. And we set about renovating the twenty dormitories and the toilets in the twenty dormitories, which took us four years.

When I first went, there were many people queuing up to help me. 'These are good people, because they want to help me', this is what I thought in the beginning. After two or three years you learned that they're helping you with their left hand, but their right hand is in your pocket. I see people for what they are now, and that goes for all people. If you don't have money to give to them or something to give them they don't want to know you anymore. And that's life, that's just the way it is. It saddens me that people I get to work there, from time to time, I have to get from Soroca, I can't get them from Badiceni. But it's a fact of life. Villages, I'm sure, are all the same, and they're all related – everyone's related to everyone else. And where we are, there are 270 people working there and I would say there's probably ten outside people that are not related to somebody there.

It's very difficult. It's really strange. It takes years, many years, as an outsider not having the language to … I suppose infiltrate is the wrong word, but to understand the people. It's hard to explain to an Irish person, but it's easy to understand having worked there. It's easy for people with money to do humanitarian aid, to work for nothing. It's very hard for people who don't have anything to work for nothing. It's also very difficult to make people believe that we as Irish people don't get paid. Nobody in Badiceni believes that I don't get paid. Nobody believes that the money will run out.

I don't have a vast amount of experience. My experience is mostly personal. Like I say, and I've said this to many Moldovan people, I come from a very humble background. My father was a shepherd and we always had food on the table. We always ate butter, but we didn't have meat. My father went to work on a bicycle until the time he retired when he was sixty-five. He brought his lunch bag, which was a small little thing, to work, and the same thing he brought home. No one ever accused him of stealing, and the police never came to our door. And people say to me the woes of Moldova and Badiceni are because people are poor. It's not because people are poor. Moldovans are as poor as we were, as I was as a child. And I understand as that was one of the things that binds me to Badiceni. I see a couple of families absolutely like we were when I was a child. Absolutely, they're just a mirror image of me fifty years ago.

People talk about the good times when it was a Russian country, and from what people say that was true, everyone had work, everyone had a job, everyone had light, everyone had heat, and now they have nothing. But it was a false job, it was all false. If we look at one institution, for argument's sake, we can see we have four electricians. This place employs four electricians, but it doesn't. It falsely employs them. A fella comes to work at eight o'clock, might work till ten o'clock and then he goes to sleep for the next twenty-two hours, and then comes home. That's not employment. That's not fulfilment. Okay, he's happy enough he can sleep for twenty-two hours or whatever he wants to sleep, but it's not fulfilment, it's not work. If you look back at your life at seventy years of age and you worked in an *internat* [boarding institution] for thirty years, what did you do for thirty years? You slept for twenty-eight of those years. That's not life, that's not what life's about. So the communist system, such as it was, employed people, but they didn't have work as such.

So when people make excuses for it – it was a communist country, people

Olesea Rosca celebrating Martisor, the festival of Spring, in Dublin in March 2008.
Photo: Niall Carson / Moldova Vision

are poor – it was a communist country and that's fair enough, but it's got nothing to do with the element of Badiceni or Moldova any more. Absolutely nothing to do with it. I don't think it's the fact that it's an institution either; it has to do with people's integrity, I think, more than anything else.

Badiceni is no different than any village in Moldova. Families are torn apart by emigration. Women – well, some men, but mostly women – go and work in foreign countries to educate their children. And then people from the villages don't have any construction skills, so if they were to go and get work they would get menial work at menial pay by unscrupulous employers in these foreign countries. Many people go and work illegally and leave big debts behind them that have to be paid – for the privilege of working in the foreign country. It costs several thousand euros for a Moldovan person to go and work in Italy or Greece, wherever it may be. Money has to be paid back at an exorbitant rate. So they leave their families behind them, with all the problems that leaves, young children with grandparents and all of that, purely because there's no employment in Moldova.

Women and parents come back from abroad and they're strangers to their children and their children are strangers to them. Their attitudes have changed, their values have changed. Children have state of the art mobile phones. They don't need these fancy telephones and that, they need a parent's love. That's not what life's about. Life's about bringing up your children, doing the best you can for your children. The Irish people did the same in the fifties; went away to England and America and worked and sent money home and made us the country that we are. That's how it was done, it was done with foreign money, not with Irish money, because there wasn't any money in Ireland. I just see people with all the material things, but they don't have the important things. It's sad, really. But there's good things in Badiceni, too.

What's the best way to help? If you could – employment. If you could, employ local people. It's the answer if you can employ local people, because you put money into the economy. We have the *internat*, which employs about 270 people, and 220 of those would come from Badiceni. Now there are probably another hundred people maybe, at the most, who would work in the town of Soroca. And then you would have another hundred people, about, working on the farm doing seasonal work. Mostly men driving tractors and sowing corn. Other than that there's no work about. The thing to do would be – if someone wants to help Moldova, do not bring humanitarian aid there, buy what you can there, if you've got the money. If you've got the money or you have the wherewithal to get the money, it's much better to buy what you want in Moldova and employ Moldovan people to do it. That's better for Moldova.

I would like to be the voice of the people, but you find that no one will listen. You can't get anyone to listen. I can get some people to listen to me, but those aren't enough. They are just being polite to a foreign person. And quite a few of the patients would confide in me, and ask me to do things I could never possibly do. They want change, they want it all, whereas they wouldn't have confided in anyone else. I want what's right for them. I want what's legally theirs, but they do not get what they're entitled to.

I'm not the Michael Kinsella that people knew years ago. I don't suffer fools anymore. Before I would have taken a lot of nonsense from people, but now I won't take it. I have different values, I see things differently, I think about things differently. I see people here who have, and I know people in Moldova who have not.

Moldova doesn't need our pity, it needs our help. I have spent a long time in Moldova, I see good and bad in Moldova, but every time I go back, we always have good experiences with people and at the end of the day that's why I keep going back. You wouldn't go there and spend the time there if you didn't like the people. Yeah, there are some really good people in Badiceni. Simple people, good people. Given the right encouragement, it's amazing what you can help Moldovans to achieve – all people, not just Moldovan.

'Have an investor mentality'
–Patricia Keane

Patricia (49) is a consultant nutritionist from Kildare. She set up **Rebuild for Bosnia** in 1998 to provide homes for displaced families following the Bosnian conflict. The organisation has provided over 100 homes in Bosnia & Herzegovina.

> ❝ I think it's a great mistake to ever think that you're a guest in their country – you're on the losing side straight away. You're not a guest in their country – you are an investor in their country. When a charity invests four or five million in a country, you are an investor so you expect and you demand your own standards. And it is a business approach. And you demand to be treated accordingly. With an investor mentality it's far more demanding. ❞

How I got involved was through a most indirect route. I went to Medugorje as a pilgrim in '98. There was an Irish girl, Paula, that was married to a Croat, and I came into contact with her and her family. They had a refugee family staying with them that had been expelled from their home. And they were living in a shack. It was a broken down, very badly broken down and old outhouse and they were living in extremely bad circumstances. Rats were running over the children at night time, it was damp, the children had asthma – they were extremely stressed. And their neighbours wanted to get some money for them to build them a house.

That's how it started. The motivation was quite simple. The motivation

The children of Afrim Myrvete with a dairy cow donated by Bóthar, Kamenica Municipality, Kosovo. *Photo: Ilirjana Ademaj / Heifer International Kosovo courtesy of Bóthar*

was to get money for this family and that was really it. We had to form the charity, obviously, to make it bona fide. But there was no other goal other than to get that money for that family. In the first fundraising session in Ireland we got money for two houses … and it just went on. One family came after another. I was always going out, from the very beginning I was going out six, seven times a year and I still am.

My experience of the conflict in Bosnia & Herzegovina was watching television and seeing what was going on, seeing the war. I just didn't understand it at the time. I just, like everybody else I saw it. It was '92 when it started so it's a long time ago and I was watching it on television and going looking at reports from Mostar. I didn't have a clue who all of these sides were, what the war was about. It was only when I got involved out there that I started to work on the research and I got a huge understanding of it then. The Irish have been going there since the apparitions began in 1982 – the first pilgrims went out a couple of years later. So, obviously during the war years they didn't go, they began going back when the war ceased. But most of them would be completely oblivious to what was going on outside of Medugorje itself. They just wouldn't come into contact with the real life, you know, with the real poverty out there. They still wouldn't know that there were refugee camps even open and existing.

People were going to their parish priests for help, and they knew of our organisation. They started then to contact us, and then we would go out and meet the families and run a full check on them and so on and then decide who we were going to help. These were ordinary people that had homes and they had land and they've never gone back. The need was for help and they were completely desperate. They were never going to have a home again. They were living in these camps. Unemployment was running at 60 per cent in some areas, with no social welfare assistance of any kind. They were very ordinary, everyday people that had come from the old plots of land, the old farms, and they were eking out a living. So there was nowhere for these people to turn to. It would have been very similar to Ireland back in the forties when there was no government aid or assistance of any kind; everybody was intensely poor. So they needed all kinds of help. They needed help with basic things, with food; they needed help with beds, a special bed for a special needs child. Just pain killers – everything. It wasn't just a house, it was everything. Their demands were huge.

We really helped everybody, everybody that was looking for help. We helped them in all kinds of ways, I remember … You know, buying – shoes, food, a wheelchair, a bed. We weren't just building houses, we put roofs back on churches, windows, got schools up and running again, functioning so that the kids could go back into school and stay there. There was one little old lady, and her son was an alcoholic, and I used to personally go out and wash her and change her every time I was there, do her nails. It was everything. It really was. The need was huge. Everybody had a need, because they had all been through war. They had injuries, they had disabilities, they needed hospital treatment, but didn't have the money. They were having to have operations without anaesthetics. So we were helping out in every way.

The home was the structure, it was the stability. And everything that's happened from there … But when we started out we never saw that that was going to happen, that was going to be a part of it. But as the years have gone by we've seen how life is stabilised for them, and these kids have gone on and had a higher level education and have done great things. It really is more than the house. When you don't have a roof over your head it really creates a huge amount of instability in the house and people break under that pressure.

There's a contract and they don't sell the houses for twenty-five years. They don't rent them, they don't start a business out of them. They don't burn them, they keep them clean, they keep them tidy, they paint the insides as well as the outsides. There are contracts. It's enforced, it has to be. They have contracts, and I have someone on the ground who works part-time for the organisation that follows everything through. It's very serious. It's: 'Patricia's coming next week so get your house in order.' And if I walk in and the house is not in order I ask them, 'Why's your house like this? This is not how you were given the house.' They're maintaining them very well, because these people lost homes, they lost precious, precious homes and, you know, these people love these new homes. They're immaculate. They are their pride and joy. They have gardens, with everything growing in them. And it's fantastic.

It's very important to use local resources. That is, materials that are resourced locally, that are made … you're talking about wood, you're talking about cement factories, you're talking about everything that can be made in the country. It's important to use local skilled tradesmen. They are the tradesmen who are trained to use the local materials, that know the best blocks and bricks for different areas, because you have to take into consideration high winds, snow. I've never brought out volunteers, never. I don't have the time to do it. I really believe in using, investing in, the local economy. I believe in using the manpower, the materials and the local knowledge. Doing it that way, you become a very credible organisation, you become a very respected organisation. You end up with a lot of contacts in local government, the best contacts in local government. We have fundraised, we've raised close to five million, and we've never done it through bringing volunteers out. We use our volunteers here, we use people here to fundraise for us.

Personally, I've learned to be very tough. I never would have been tough in my life, but I've learned to be very, very tough. Really, having to be so firm about people, and getting very good deals on contracts and negotiations and having to hit very hard when work has not been done – really be the boss. That was all exceptionally challenging for me. But I became that person. I got a huge amount of respect for it. And I have great relationships with the people, really, very good relationships. I'd be known to be very fair, and I'd be known to be fastidious in what I do, committed and reliable. But tough.

Tough, being you really having to follow up on things even in a conflictual way or a non-conflictual way, when things have not been done the way they should have been done. It's a very male-orientated society out there, and they think they can get away with whatever they want to get away with – they will lie to you, they will, and they will try and get out of it. You can be taken for a ride, a very expensive one. It's really taking a very firm stand – that's what I had to learn to do. That was all very new for me. You just have to do it. It's like getting up on that bicycle and you know you're going to fall off, and you know when you fall off you're going to get hurt. And you get back on it a second time and you know how it's going to be and you know that fall is going to be tough, but you know you have to do it. It's simply deciding you have to do it. Regardless of the fallout.

I was the person in control of spending the money and the money was always spent in the way it should have been spent. But it's jobs not being done properly; it's the standard of work not being up to the standard that was written in contract. It was work being unfinished. That's when you have to go in and fight hard. I'll give you an example: one project being built in Mostar, it was an English architect that was over the job. He told the builders to take down a wall, he said, 'That wall isn't right, take that wall down.' He told the men sixteen times to take the wall down, and they didn't take the wall down. The seventeenth time he went in, and he had to take the wall down himself. He took a pickaxe to the wall and put so many holes in the wall that the wall fell. And that's what you have to do to be hard. That's typical of what happens and that's when – what do you do? You take a pickaxe in your hand and you take it down yourself and then they get it.

The first thing that you learn is when things have to be dealt with, they have to be dealt with and you have to recognise that fact and go with it. And challenging people is never the way to be popular, but that's not the point. The point is that they have been given something, they have been asked to do something, and it should be done to the expected standards.

I think it's a great mistake to ever think that you're a guest in their country – you're on the losing side straight away. You're not a guest in their country – you are an investor in their country. When a charity invests four or five million in a country, you are an investor so you expect and you demand your own standards. You bring enough money to a country and you're investing in homes and the community and you're creating jobs and out of that people are making a living and they're building their own homes and they're putting a new roof on their house and they're repairing and building whole facets to their homes and you're bringing in that money – you are an investor. And it is a business approach. And you demand to be treated accordingly. With an investor mentality it's far more demanding.

That was something that I learned in the very early days – that this was business and it had to be treated like business. Yes, you can have informalities and you can have your laugh with them and you can have a meal with them and you can have a drink with them, but at the end of the day it's business. It's not about charity, it's about business, because it's your damn money. It's someone else's money and you are the caretaker of that person's money. You are the bursar; you are responsible for your donor's money. They have entrusted that money to you, so it's business.

Every hundred euro you can save is a hundred euro less that you don't have to work for, that's how I negotiate deals all the time, and you fight for it hard and you fight for as much as you can get off that. You start off high and you work down and you come down to what two people are happy with. But you have to work hard first. The builder, the contractor that I use in Bosnia & Herzegovina, he said, 'Of all the people I've ever had to deal with, you are the toughest of all.' You get tough like that. You also get the confidence in doing it, you know you can do it nicely and in a really nice way and get the desired result without someone feeling they have been railroaded.

It's having the right contacts as well. The groundwork has to be done. The initial groundwork has to be done in establishing the right contacts on the ground. That is the key factor in setting up an organisation outside of the country. Don't be deluded into thinking you know it all and you can do it. That's a huge mistake. Because the national people know the ropes, they know the pitfalls, they know the loops. They know what they can get away with and what they can't, and they know how to twist things, manipulate things. I think it's essential to proceed with caution and to proceed very slowly. The vital thing is to contact the non-national NGO on the ground and who is established and who has been there. I think that people going out for the first time don't contact the established NGOs on the ground. It's a huge mistake, but people have pride and they act out of that pride. But a good businessman … he is not going to have much pride, because he has his own investment to be concerned about. He's the one who is going to be in touch with someone who's established. He's the one who would put his nose to the ground and say, 'I am willing to take you on, I'm willing to consult with you.'

The homes go beyond what you do now, it goes beyond this generation. It affects many generations to come. What I've learned is the unseen ... what I never envisaged or I never thought would happen or could happen. It wasn't just putting a roof over someone's head, it was all the ripples that that was going to create. It was. It's not just the mother or the father or the widow, it's the next generation – it's their children, it's their children's children. This home is going to be there for generations. That hope that we gave them, which led to an education, is going to ... the effect of that is going to be there, because without that help they wouldn't have had the education. They now know the importance of that education, where it has brought them; that's going to impact their children and their children's children.

'Educate across the board'
–Mairie Cregan

Mairie (49) is a social worker and lecturer in Cork. An experienced foster carer and adoptive parent herself, she founded **Aurelia Trust** in 1994 to support the development of fostering in Romania. She has also been involved in fostering programmes and training in Belarus and Russia.

> I'd always say their needs there are no different to what they are here. I suppose I used to think institutionalisation was a Romanian problem; now I know it's international, it's universal, and it's just that the numbers were so vast in Romania, the care was so basic. Absolute poverty, and lack of education, definitely, but who do you educate? You'd have to educate across the board, including the policy makers and then the people who would be the objects of it.

I started out in Romania in 1990 in the very early days. It was – how do I want to put it? – literally like nothing we'd ever seen, the deprivation that those children suffered. The nearest thing that the reporters that I met out there said, would have been the liberation of the camps after the war. So I think we were totally unprepared for what we needed to do; the aid that was taken into a lot of the institutions was robbed, so the children did not benefit and nobody had an organised plan. It was a very ad hoc, I suppose, response to the situation. But you have to cast your mind back – none of us even knew where Romania was on the map when we went out there, and it was really a heart response, just to try and alleviate some of the suffering of the children.

But we did not understand the level of deprivation and the damage that was done to those kids. When we started out we thought it would be a matter of clean clothes, clean water, and all of that is very important. But once the children were receiving the physical care they needed, the actual disabilities became visible. It then became very visible, you know, the fact that they had been damaged hugely by their early-years experience, by the appalling deprivation that they had experienced.

I came as a foster carer/trainer, but there weren't that many of us. I'd been a foster carer since 1983 and my mother fostered from before I was born. So that was what we were bringing to Romania ... but looking at what was going on there, there was no way that fostering could have happened for the kids who'd already experienced the hell and the horror of the orphanages. So I started with the younger children. We thought it was a matter of just recruiting foster carers, but of course it wasn't. I remember being at a conference in Bucharest in '91, and I think there was about half an hour of arguing by interpreters about how to translate the word 'foster care'. So that's the level we were at, there was very little informal foster care either.

The community had broken down, and Ceausescu's answer to any organised community activism was to break up the village communities and move them into the high rise flats and buildings, where they had no sewerage, they had no running water a lot of the time, no electricity – or if they had, they had it for a few hours a day. It is very hard to see the thriving and vibrant country that Romania is now and to imagine the level of deprivation at that time. If you don't have a community looking out for you then you can do what you want, so it was easy enough to abandon children, because there was no one to (a) support you or (b) to condemn you if you gave your child into the institution.

So we started the first foster care project then for disabled children. That took an awful lot of training, and the recruitment of the foster carers took a long time. The foster carers were supported for two years – they got huge support, they got twenty-four-hour support, and it worked. We did a lot of training in Bucharest University; the first few classes were with social workers. We did a lot of training with the social workers. We started a group home and started modularising the orphanage where we worked to try and create a more home-like atmosphere around it. Institutions, the problem with them is that if you have lived in them long enough, you can't live anywhere else.

Staff member Nutzi in *Casa Aurelia* group home for adults with disabilities in Lazu near Constanta, Romania. *Photo: John Mulligan / Aurelia Trust.*

We've seen that in Ireland, where our homelessness has gone through the roof for vulnerable people, because we closed down a lot of our mental hospitals. We put forward care in the community without asking ourselves if the community care. You know, they are frightened of people with psychiatric issues and disabilities. So we had to look at that in Romania and so our answer to that was, look, rather than make them all homeless, let's modularise the institutions into apartments. That worked very well, you know, they had a better life.

Fostering is one of the most difficult of enterprises; it's breaking down all over the world, often because those in charge are trying to intellectualise it and they are also trying to professionalise it to such a point that it won't work. What we try to do would be to locate ourselves down at the ground level, which is hands-on care. A lot of the time that's looked down on. We've worked over the years, and especially the early days, with organisations who took Western styles of care and imposed them on Romania, and mainly they didn't work. Nobody asked the Romanians, 'What do you want?' No one asked the families what they wanted and it was automatically assumed, this attitude of neo-colonialism, just assuming that we know better. You know, a lot of the time all they want is to get through the day like us.

When I started working there at first I couldn't stand the carers in the orphanage; I mean, I was very young, only twenty-eight, and I think, really, I was very arrogant. I was very hurt, really upset, and didn't understand. I asked one care worker, 'How can you watch these children in the cold?' She said, 'But they don't feel the cold.' I mean, I realise now, through my own training, that what was happening there was they had to dehumanise the children or they wouldn't have been able to cope. I would be quite ashamed now of the way I behaved and what I thought then, I just didn't understand or couldn't – it's just so hard. Some of our volunteers now weren't even born when I went out there, and trying to explain what it was like – and why we behaved the way we did – is very hard.

I think once they saw that we were genuine and wanted or hoped that the kids could have a better life, we started getting on better with the carers. Also, I started telling them about my own children, or whatever, and you'd find common ground, and might be the same age as somebody, but she looked twice as old as you, you know their lives are very difficult. But once we found common ground and individual volunteers started making relationships, then it did improve. But they were such a ground-down group of women in the orphanage, and then in the villages their lives were just so bleak, you know, and then you've these Westerners coming in telling them what to do. We would have spent a week's wages, for them, on our evening meal. We didn't have sensitivity around that.

The training plan initially, was to go in, recruit, support and train foster parents and the authorities, to make sure they carried out the training needed by foster carers, that they understand that an institutionalised child would not behave the way a family child will, and how you have to understand that. You go in with your eyes open and not setting everybody up for failure. They need, especially older children, if they're from institutions and have experienced early life adversity, they need huge support, and so do the parents who are going to care for them. So it's not the easy option people think it is. They think Mammy and Daddy will love them and everything is going to be okay – it's not. It's going to be okay for a while, and then if the placement breaks down the child has failed again … so you just have to be careful. Go slow and go right.

One of the issues we are dealing with now is that we recruited older women as foster parents originally. They are too old now to keep the children who are now adults and are special needs adults. So we are left with a problem that we did not foresee earlier on. And I mean, that was a huge lesson. We don't always have the answers, but at least we've the questions this time, which we didn't have last time. So we learned to look at the consequences, and I think we had too many short term responses and if I had anything to pass on, it would be to look at the long term, ten years time, fifteen years time, and the impact of your work in the years ahead, because I never thought of twenty years time, or that I would still be involved in Romania so many years on

Recently, the orphanage we worked in has re-opened under a different name for adults. We got our kids out and that's a very good thing and they did up the wing, before moving in new clients, but it's still very bad. These people have to go somewhere and they are so institutionalised. I suppose in its latter years, and you would be shot for saying this, the orphanage wasn't the worst place to be. You had your little apartments. They had programmes going. There were three organisations involved there and they worked very well together, and there was a better life there compared to what they had at the start.

So that is why when we hear of institutions going to be closed we want to make sure that those kids aren't on the streets in six months, because that is what is happening. So we would be very mindful of that, you just have to do it slowly, thoroughly, and you have to have a team that can agree to disagree and try something and come back, and not be afraid to take criticism. You just have to take the best of the ideas, and then just don't make the same mistakes again. At least we're asking the questions now.

I'd always say their needs there are no different to what they are here. I suppose I used to think institutionalisation was a Romanian problem; now I know it's international, it's universal, and it's just that the numbers were so vast in Romania, the care was so basic. Absolute poverty, and lack of education, definitely, but who do you educate? You'd have to educate across the board, including the policy makers and then the people who would be the objects of it. I think in Romania it was just absolute poverty that caused it, because where it's been put in – where foster care is good in Romania it's among the best there is – probably one of the best foster care projects I've seen in the world has been in Romania.

I think we're there because we're allowed to help. If I was allowed to do half in Ireland what I do in Romania, I wonder would I be as busy in Romania, but I wouldn't be allowed into a unit here and rightly so. People can arrive in Romania and if they get on with the mayor or local officials, they can do what they want in a hospital or an orphanage, and that's not right. And I'd imagine that sometimes the Romanians think of our own care system, and they would just be thinking. 'Oh, it's no great shakes what you have either. Why are you minding us here when your suicide rate is the third highest in Europe for youth?' You know, why aren't we looking at other stuff in Ireland? Some of our long-stay mental hospitals are appalling, you know, so I sometimes wonder why they don't just tell us to get out, and sort our own country …

Fostering is there internationally. We're not the pioneers, but we have accelerated the process in Romania. They are hungry for education, and especially people who study abroad and come back, they are the ones I find now that could be in an office and after a meeting they will come and find you and latch on to you asking about a theoretical framework for doing this, that or the other. That is very heartening, you know, that they see there is another way. Our greatest gift, I think, is that we are bringing expertise and we are enabling, through training.

'Do your research'

–Tom McEnaney

Tom (43) is a journalist and media consultant from Dublin. He first travelled to Belarus in 1998 and subsequently set up **International Orphanage Development Programme** to support disadvantaged children in Belarus, India, Haiti and other countries around the world.

> Go off, do your research, talk to people; it doesn't mean doing academic research, it doesn't even necessarily mean doing a report. When we were doing farms it was all about talking to people. Talk to the collective farms, we talked to them about what should be done in the orphanages and they had great advice. It's amazing. If you go looking for money, you'll find it's hard work. If you go looking for advice, it might have as great an impact as the money you'll raise, but it's much easier to get.

I went over to Belarus for the *Sunday Tribune* to write an article about one of the first Irish groups which was taking on a substantial project with an institution in Belarus. I found out about the trip, and being an engineer by background, I was intrigued and I decided to go along. Belarus was my first big work. I had in college been involved in Vincent de Paul and headed up a group which did work with disadvantaged children and old folks, but when I got into journalism I kind of cut it out, because if you're a journalist you can't be involved on the matters you're reporting on. But here was an opportunity – because it was abroad – so I decided, okay, I'll go over.

Because I'd only known about Belarus from the publicity, I went over with the impression that there were a very large number of disabled children and disabled people in Belarus. I expected to see people with disabilities on every street corner, you know, and I was amazed to find out that by and large, Belarusians were very much like the Irish people and there was, in the orphanages in particular, there was considerable poverty. So I came back to Ireland, wrote my article ... and I remember that there was one child in particular, Dima, a nine-year-old that was in the classroom next to the room that I was doing up, and he used to come and see me every day ... I remember one day when I was really down, you know it was two weeks that I was out there and it was hard work. I was kind of going, 'What the hell am I doing here?' And he arrived at the door of the gym with a big bunch of geranium blossoms that he'd picked for me, and I just thought, 'Yeah, this is why I'm here.' So I finished the article, saying to Dima and all the children ...my only message is that I will be back, so I decided that I would go back and see if I could help.

After a while, I realised I wanted to concentrate on figuring out ways of helping as many orphanages as possible ... I just wanted to take on my own orphanage, because I reckoned that the opposite law of diminishing returns is law of increasing returns. If you pick great need you can get great return for what you put in. We were not in the business of having trophy orphanages or the best orphanages in the country or anything like that. We were about trying to raise the mean for everybody. If we were getting to the stage where we were able to put second showers in an orphanage, then it was time to move on, it was time to find an orphanage that needed a first set of showers. The way I explain it to people is that if you go into an orphanage that doesn't have showers and you give them showers, you give the children the ability to clean themselves. When you put in a second set of showers, you just give the children a choice between where they clean themselves. So I preferred to go for the very worst orphanages and I preferred to go for institutions that nobody else is helping, because if you go there the need is always great and you can get great bang for your buck. You can have an impact on the lives of a lot of children relatively cheaply.

Until we were a reasonably substantial organisation, I never dealt with government, because I would have gotten mired in bureaucracy and it would have been impossible to work. Instead I dealt with the orphanages,

Tom McEnaney from Dublin with children in the playground of a residential centre for deaf children in Belarus. *Photo: International Orphanage Development Programme.*

and I found out what worked effectively up to a point. We would go into an orphanage, and I'd recommend this to anybody, is don't go in and say you're going to do things this way or that way or whatever. Go in, ask them what they need. Go in a support capacity. Sit down with the director of an orphanage, and my technique was this: under-promise and over-deliver. Belarus is littered with institutions that can tell you about charities who turned up and promised them the sun, moon and stars and didn't deliver. So our priority, our thing was always under-promise, over-deliver.

The first orphanage we took on – Dyatlovo – we spent about 300 grand on it. We did a huge number of projects on it over a number of years. Things like roof, gutters, windows, internal plastering, new farm, things, anything from tampons to chisels, you know. And then I decided very quickly, you know, that this has worked so well, let's try and bring every orphanage in Belarus up to a certain standard. So although we much prefer to see no institutions, as is international best practice, the fact is that in the meantime, children are still there and just turning your eye on them and having a wordy aspiration is no help to children who are in orphanages that don't have access to showers, that don't have access to play and they don't have proper food.

And I found of all the projects in terms of high impact, cost effective things you could do for disadvantaged children, if you give them access to play that's a brilliant thing to do – so we put in a playground at the first orphanage and within three days they were different children; of all the things I've done in the last thirteen years, this was the most amazing difference I've ever seen. Literally before our eyes the children turned from being dull and lifeless into being full of the joys of life and laughing, wherever they went, not just in the playground, but throughout the orphanage.

So because the playground project worked very well, I decided to put playgrounds into all the orphanages in Belarus. I started off by reading about play, reaffirmed my own personal experience, you know … So everything I read said play is amazing, so I said, okay, we have to put playgrounds in all the orphanages. If I can have this much of a difference with one bloody playground! So we said, if we're going to do that, we have to assess every orphanage, so I got a team of people that went over for three months and they went round physically assessing sixty orphanages. I didn't like the idea of bringing over the playgrounds, so I found a factory in Minsk and I negotiated a really good deal with them on playgrounds. So we went off and went around our businesspeople in Ireland and raised a quarter of a million and put in the playgrounds.

That took about two years, and then in the meantime we'd done our assessments, we'd moved on to another orphanage, we'd picked the worst one, and then the next worst and so on. We would do Santa Claus with them as a way of keeping tabs on the orphanage, the ones that we were developing. So we redeveloped eleven institutions in Belarus by raising funds through doing Santa Claus … I've done about twenty-five trips now, brought about 120 people over and we've been doing Santa now for the last thirteen years.

They're not stupid. They're Russian or Belarusian, call them what you will. Belarus is one of the most cultured and educated countries in the world. They have a parallel system of paediatric care and psychiatric care which is at least the equivalent of the Western systems. It's just resources they need. We bring in very, very little new thinking. There are some small exceptions to that, but they are exceptional. And where we do bring in new thinking, usually we've taken it from different orphanages. We had an orphanage that said, 'We really like transition apartments; we'd like to put in an apartment which children can stay in for three months and get used to feeding themselves and cooking for themselves.' I loved the idea, so we funded it, and then everywhere else we went, we suggested transition apartments, and everywhere we went, they went for it. So okay, we were bringing in an idea, but it was a Belarusian idea.

We've put in about six hundred-acre farms now with orphanages, and that for me is sustainable, because you're making a sustained difference. As I define sustainable, it means by and large we never introduced anything in the country … so all our tractors, all our machinery, all our beds, everything is sourced locally. That's sustainable. Buy locally; if something breaks down they know how to fix it. They're able to get the parts for it, not foreign parts. Don't be going buying German machinery and saying, 'Oh, we'll give them the best Massey Ferguson'. Even if the local material is not as good, it's often much more cost effective to be sourcing it locally than to be paying transporting it.

Originally we consulted far and wide about what should be in the farms. And we looked at different strains of potato and everything else, and we talked to … honestly, people who knew more about spuds than anybody you've ever met. And we decided we weren't going to introduce any methods or any vegetables or any even types of vegetables. Everything had to be based on the best available locally. So when we got to an orphanage, we'd find out what's growing locally, what's the expertise locally, and then we'd apply that to the orphanage. So we'd go to the collective farm, see what they're growing, and then you'd know that this farm was very good at growing carrots, spuds and cabbage – we'd never tell them what they're growing.

We had a strict rule that we would only ever, that we would never fund staff, only fund capital projects, and only fund it where there is a pre-existing ability to fund staff themselves. For a while we were funding staff in India, but we stopped. We now fund everything on a joint basis. We still give them assistance, but it's just: 'Don't ever fund staff. Don't develop dependency.' … you know, work with local authorities, let them put in staff, let them provide the food, the ongoing current costs, don't deal with current costs – capital projects are the way to go, that's one thing that I've learned hugely.

So there we were, we've had the basis for a plan, and thirteen years later, some of the orphanages we've worked with closed down. The building hasn't been closed down, some of them have been turned into boarding schools, they've all been turned into something else that's child-related, but the orphanage systems are actually being closed down on the directive of the president. So moving on, over time, now we got to the point where the physical need in orphanages isn't that great. We were picking up the worst ones, so the ones that were left were ones that were closer to a mean anyway, and at the same time there were loads of other organisations working with orphanages and putting in help ...

So we have a number of challenges now; one of them is to redefine or refocus ourselves in the way that actually facilitates the closing down of orphanages, the other one is to try and ... do that in a way that promotes the development of an NGO sector and a culture of philanthropy within Belarus itself. We're now working on a house that we're in the middle of buying, a nice big house, and there's a couple who currently foster three children, they're moving into it and we're going to add five children. And two of the children will be siblings of a little seven-year-old girl that they look after, her brother and sister are currently in an orphanage – they'll be living with her and it's a wonderful family, and I think that's exactly the way it should be happening. The way we worked it was we paid some of the cost, a Belarusian philanthropist paid some of the cost, and an Italian charity came in and paid some of the cost, and the local authority had to pay as much as any charity, so the local authority had to contribute to the project so they owned it from the beginning. So we're trying to put together a model, and the idea is we want to build 100 of these houses.

One of my principles: prove it, do it well, do it small; if you make a mistake, it hasn't cost you a fortune and you haven't put people out in a huge way. Do it small, but do it well. Replicate it, prove that you're capable of doing it twice, then scale it. If you do two, why not do 200? Scale! You have to do scale! If you're capable, you know ... Don't be afraid of thinking big. The difference between people who change the world and people who don't is that people who change the world decide that they can. But don't go and just act big straight away ... And try and figure out projects that you can scale from the off. Identify, if you've got ten projects available to you and you're trying to figure out which one you can do, do the one that you might be capable of scaling so you have at least given yourself the possibility of scaling it, even if you decide later on that you don't necessarily want to do it.

I think it's reasonable for small, versatile charities to define the response subjectively. If you're a big NGO, then you must define your response objectively, but if you're a small, responsive organisation, it's quite okay to define your response according to your own abilities. So you go along and say, 'Listen, we're an organisation, we're particularly good at disability' – well, that's perfectly fine for you just to focus in on disability; if you happen to love kites, then it's perfectly reasonable to turn around and say, 'Okay, I want to help children have kites.' When it comes to most things in life, including philanthropy, there is no objective truth, there is only subjective response.

Now, that said, that said, it is incumbent on all of us to be aspiring to best international practice. And if you're going to help, you have a responsibility to help as effectively as you can, and so you must at least know what best international practice is, even if you then choose to ignore it, but you have a responsibility not to act in ignorance. The best way of making sure you don't make mistakes is to do research. If you're going to be figuring out what is the best way of doing what you do, the first way is to say, 'Okay, who has done this already?' Go off, do your research, talk to people; it doesn't mean doing academic research, it doesn't even necessarily mean doing a report. When we were doing farms it was all about talking to people. Talk to the collective farms, we talked to them about what should be done in the orphanages and they had great advice. It's amazing. If you go looking for money, you'll find it's hard work. If you go looking for advice, it might have as great an impact as the money you'll raise, but it's much easier to get.

The world is globalised, we can now see need in Zimbabwe as easily if not more easily than we can see it down the road. But our response to that hasn't moved. The way in which we think about charity hasn't kept up with globalisation, I don't believe. If you're helping somebody, you should help according to need, surely, or according to your ability to deliver, but not according to whether they're black or Christian or Irish or Jewish or you know? Belarus is a developed country. But Ireland is a developed country, and there's still need. If a child is cold and hungry and needs help, it doesn't really matter if it's a cold hungry child in a rich country or a cold hungry child in a poor country, you know. I'm now looking at ways I can help other children in Ireland, so I'm trying to establish where the need is. I could see myself in the morning helping children in America, no problem, if I thought I could make an effective difference and I saw a real need.

I tried not doing this for a while and I was terribly unhappy. This is what fills the empty space; this is what defines who it is I am when I wake up in the morning. I think, and again this is for me, first of all my personal, my philosophical answer to the question is that I believe all of us have the responsibility to improve the lives of others according to their need and according to our ability. If I have the capacity to put in sixty playgrounds, but I only put in five, I am not entitled to pat myself on the back and go, 'Aren't I brilliant, I've put in five playgrounds'. I'm not preaching to anybody else and I would never say this to anybody else, but this is a conversation I have to myself. This is a personal journey. If I'm not operating to the maximum of my capacity, then I've failed.

'Deal with the right people'
–Fiona Corcoran

Fiona (45) became involved in the Chernobyl relief effort and left her job in banking in 1995 to establish **Greater Chernobyl Cause** in Cork. The organisation supports various partners and social services, including hospices, orphanages and day centres, in Ukraine and Kazakhstan.

> 66 Do not start giving money out to people running orphanages or running care centres – you can't do that, because you don't know where the money's going to go. You have to deal with the right people. I would advise anyone to forge working relationships with credible groups on the ground. You can't just arrive in a country. 99

I began … I suppose it was back in 1995. I read an article in the *Evening Echo* about the airlift of four children from the Chernobyl affected area of Belarus to Cork for medical treatment. And I can remember saying to my flatmate at the time, 'Let's just go and see these kids, because they're in a foreign land.' They were in a hospital not far from us, and from then I just got involved in a rota for visiting the children. I felt it must be terrible for these kids, being in a strange country, without any parents. And I became very close to all the children, especially to a little girl. Two weeks later, she died, and it turned my world round completely.

After that I became involved then in work in Belarus and Ukraine. Then in 1999, I can remember receiving a telephone call from a Dublin businessman who had read an article. There was a child featured in this article, and he

Tessa O'Connor from Co. Clare with one of the residents in Rudyna, a residential setting for older adults in Belarus (2010). *Photo: Maurice Gunning / Burren Chernobyl Project.*

said, 'We need to get this child to Ireland for surgery, and I will help you,' and so I said, 'Okay.' I saw that it was in Kazakhstan, and I had no idea where Kazakhstan was. I knew it was former USSR, but I had no idea where it was located. So with the help of our government, and working then with the Kazakh government, the object was just to bring this child back to Ireland for surgery. And even though I'd been working in Belarus and Ukraine, and I thought I had an idea of what suffering was … but I don't think anything could have prepared me for the suffering or the devastation that I came across – the smell of vomit, singed hair, urine, it was an overpowering stench. And there was this one child – he was eighteen months, the child, but he looked five or six months because of the malnutrition. I remember leaving with him clutched in my arms, and I said to the lady in the orphanage that we would be back, and she said, 'No, people come and people go, but they don't come back – we're too far away.' And that really struck me, and I thought, 'oh God, we have to go back and help these people.'

And we did a few months later, thanks to the support of people back home, and we renovated the baby home and brought it into the twenty-first century. Then we discovered that was a feeder home – like a primary school is a feeder school – this was a feeder home to an orphanage. So I went to visit, and it was a hellhole, literally, toilets outside, temperatures drop to about minus forty and they had absolutely nothing there, it was appalling. So okay, we thought we had to do something there, because what was the point in supporting the baby home there but then allowing them to go at the age of five to this place?

We've supported many Irish couples down through the years adopting from Kazakhstan and Ukraine. But it is a very difficult process. These baby homes are a result of welfare parents, of – let's say – unmarried mums, because they are not able to keep their babies. And that's what changed in Ireland and what I truly believe was the reason orphanages closed in Ireland. Number one, they have the money to care for the baby alone, and number two, there's no longer stigma attached with single parents, absolutely not, but in these countries – yeah. They don't have money to care for the children solely and secondly, the stigma is there, and I suppose it's hard. And thirdly, these children are born with deformities and challenges and so on and so forth and they just can't cope.

Sadly, the children will end up in care, and what happens from a very young age is that the mother is relinquished of her rights – her rights are taken from her or she just gives up her rights. She left the baby at the hospital and she leaves through no fault of her own. Some of the couples there are saying to me, 'Will you take this letter, and will you give this letter now to the orphanage and make sure to put it in the child's file, because the mum will come back some day.' The people in the homes and institutions, they kind of look at us and say, 'Don't be so ridiculous, the mothers will never come back for them.' But I said, 'You should see now, in Ireland it's now about tracing the parents and tracing the children of those who were adopted all those years ago.'

There are so many children on the streets of Ukraine. What happens is they run away from the orphanages, from the homes, because they might be physically, sexually, mentally abused, and they end up on the streets, and I think they end up running and they're going to face new dangers; they think it's a sanctuary, but there's no sanctuary on the streets, because there's child prostitution, trafficking, they end up abusing solvents, like glue, and that can lead to eventual death.

So what we did there is we joined forces with a group called Father's House in Kiev. What we're trying to do there is put a break in the cycle of the children living on the streets. We have young foster parents, but they essentially give up two years of their life to look after maybe six or seven former street children, so they start the first years of married life with these six or seven children. The kids get care, first of all, and for the first time, they're forging friendships with adults, and with their peers, and it's trust, really, at the end of the day, first and foremost. And they're placed there in foster homes for two years initially, but the eventual aim is adoption. Not adoption abroad, but adoption there. Why take them away if there is a hope of them living there in their own country?

I think a lot of Irish charities would have been involved in sending aid in the beginning and they'd have progressed to greater things, like huge building projects and hoping that the orphanages would have closed down. In the end that's going to be a long, long time, because – just speaking about our own organisation – remember, the majority of children we work with, especially in Kazakhstan, are mentally challenged. So they're not going to be fostered, sadly, they're not going to be adopted. So somebody said to me – that's ridiculous, building a new orphanage, it'll be gone in five or ten years. It won't be gone in five or ten years, simply because: who's going to care for the children? There's a different mentality there. At the end of the day, as well here in Ireland, people do not adopt or foster children with these mental challenges. So when people say, 'We want to close down all the orphanages', for us, that's not a reality.

We've developed good contacts over the years. In Kazakhstan we work with the United Nations Development Programme. But we work alongside the government in both countries, which is very important … whatever you feel about the red tape and the bureaucracy. But we have developed, despite that, very good relations with the government of both countries, so work is easier now than it was in the beginning. The majority of people I would work closely with would be my friends now, like volunteer colleagues over there. I suppose the trust and the belief we have in each other and working close with each other for so many years – it's together that we've actually put these projects together. It's together we've managed to place the children in care in their own countries or even bring the children here to Ireland for medical reasons. And it's true that it's through the people on the ground that we're able to achieve that.

Overall, yeah, it's been a great experience, and sure, you come across people down through the years or whatever that you think are great and wonderful that prove to be otherwise. It rarely happens, but it does from time to time. But it happens all over the world, it does. You can't continue relations with these people then, because the one thing is you've got to be 100 per cent sure; you've got to have 100 per cent transparency and accountability. We have to be sure that the money's spent wisely, and that's why we've got the people on the ground, you know, and you're watching, you're constantly monitoring everything.

Do not start giving money out to people running orphanages or running care centres – you can't do that, because you don't know where the money's going to go. You have to deal with the right people. I would advise anyone to forge working relationships with credible groups on the ground. You can't just arrive in a country. I received a call there from a guy recently and he said, 'Hey, I'm going in to do this risk assessment thing in Kyrgyzstan, can you give me advice?' I said, 'Well, who's meeting you? Where are you going, who are you staying with, who are you working with, how are you going to begin this risk assessment?' He said, 'Well, I'm not really sure.' There's huge unrest there, but this guy is going into this country with no backup, with no people on the ground, no agency on the ground that he was dealing with. I said, 'Well, first of all, talk to the UNDP'; the UNDP have offices in most countries around the world. You can speak to our foreign affairs, you speak to the Irish embassy in Moscow if you're going to Kazakhstan or Kyrgyzstan, so that's very important. You speak to our Irish embassy, you speak to foreign affairs, you speak to the UNDP, you speak to groups like ourselves, that's what I would advise. Talk to these various groups before you even begin to work there. Or if there are agencies or charities or NGOs that work there go to those people and see them.

Some people do say, 'Have you spread yourself too thin?' But I don't think so, because, you know, it's very hard to say no when you realise that if you don't help, there's no one else to support these people, and if you don't support them, they may not survive. If somebody had said to me eleven years ago, 'In a decade you will have managed to do A, B, C and D', I would say impossible, absolutely impossible to do so much. So I guess it's what we've achieved as a people. And you keep going and you must keep going, because you can't leave this neglect. You must not ... we must not let people wallow in this neglect.

'The direct approach is best'

−Tajma Kapic & Svenn Braamark

Tajma (45) moved to Ireland in 1993 from Bosnia & Herzegovina and works as Project Director for **Cradle**. Svenn (56) moved from Norway to Ireland in 1998 and is Executive Director of Cradle. Cradle was originally set up within the music industry in Ireland in 1992 to deliver aid to the Balkans during the Bosnian war.

> You are much better off going through a local group – ask somebody if they know a local NGO or a local organisation. There are different societies of parents or local groups who also do marvellous stuff in all of these countries. You can go through them and so you avoid corruption. Obviously, the United Nations, UNDP, bilateral aid does whatever they do – but for smaller NGOs the direct approach is best. *Tajma Kapic*

Tajma: I am from Bosnia & Herzegovina. I got involved in development work during the war. I was working in a local NGO and I was distributing food around town and across the front line – food that we got from many organisations from Ireland and around the world, including Cradle. That's how I got involved. So basically, I was on the receiving end of aid, and therefore I think that – because of my personal experience – I think we have that special sensitivity of working with people. I think Cradle always deals with people in a way that I would like to have people deal with me. I remember when we started getting aid in Bosnia & Herzegovina and you opened the truck and all you would see is somebody cleaning out their wardrobe and sending the stuff. And so even though I had been in the war for two years, I refused to wear anything else but my own trousers that I bought in Italy the year before the war, because I bought it myself and because that is also about dignity. You can be hungry, but you know, you don't have to be hungry and humiliated at the same time, and that is why dignity is so important. I've been in Cradle since I arrived in Ireland in October of 1993, and I have been working and helping ever since, really. Well, in my case, I didn't really choose, I think this type of work has chosen me. It became my career by default, but I am happy for it.

Cradle started with direct aid and emergency trucks. In 1992 and 1993, all through 1995, I think that Cradle sent a truck a month. We go with emergency aid and we've sent several thousand tonnes of aid by now. It started from this direct emergency aid for kids through our baby care appeal. You know, we sent the trucks out on O'Connell Street or the top of Grafton Street, collecting nappies and food and goods, mostly for kids, because we are a children's charity. Basically then, after that, after the first wave of emergency aid, we started thinking about more long-term approaches. We started looking into therapy through art and music. We set up a violin project where we help kids deal with trauma through music, and also our art workshop. We also have our student support programme to pay for kids to go to university, because their families didn't have any income.

One of the projects that we have done that I think makes a huge impact is the sport project, because it has mostly girls involved and because I believe sports are so good for people, although I know it's not food and it's not direct assistance. I played handball for years, and I believe that is a huge part of educating you as well, because my handball playing helped me loads even in my work and everything. Helping with sharing and team work, in not being afraid of fighting for things I believe in or afraid to ask for help. All of that. It's so important. It teaches you also to share with people, but also not to be afraid to ask if you need help or support. If you do team sports from an early age that's what you learn.

In 1999, we extended our work after the Kosovo crisis to Kosovo and Albania. We had an emergency programme there as well. We sent a group of performers to a refugee camp in Albania, not just to entertain the children, but to teach them about fighting and mines and the dangers of mines. We have been involved with that region ever since. We took our work to South

Irish volunteers who took part in a week long 'Women's Build' in 2010, to construct a house for a family in Pitesti, Romania. *Photo: Habitat for Humanity Ireland.*

East Asia after the tsunami, but our main work is still within the Balkans.

Unfortunately, I have to say in the case of Bosnia & Herzegovina, if you really look at the economic situation of the country and the majority of people now – and obviously because I am from the region, and wherever I go I speak to people – I would say people need emergency aid now more than before. More and more people are accessing communal kitchens now and the number of older people applying for a meal a day is increasing. Those older people were saying how they had it much better during the war, because there were loads of agencies around and there was lots of aid and now there is nothing, really. Once the crisis is passed it's very difficult to get any money or aid or anything for the country. People go from one crisis region to another in order to get money for the projects, and then people whose countries happen to be off the news are left with nothing. It really saddens me that every time that I go there I see how many more people are really hungry and are reduced to not even having food.

In Cradle we only employ local personnel. So we are in touch with the local community constantly about what's happening. That's one thing. The second thing is that Cradle always – somehow we have managed though all these years to avoid red tape, so we are dealing directly with people and working with people and we get the information on what is happening. For me personally, again because it's my country, I feel very conscious about the working of the whole system. For me, relating to problems of corruption in many countries, including Bosnia & Herzegovina, I know I can go and look all our sponsors in the eye and say, 'Many people gave us money and the money has gone to the right place.' Because I did it. It is directed through local representatives. It doesn't go to a third party of any kind.

You are much better off going through a local group – ask somebody if they know a local NGO or a local organisation. There are different societies of parents or local groups who also do marvellous stuff in all of these countries. You can go through them and so you avoid corruption. Obviously, the United Nations, UNDP, bilateral aid does whatever they do – but for smaller NGOs the direct approach is best. We can make a difference to some people's lives this way. I know, because I saw it. Especially for a smaller NGO, the direct approach is a good approach.

I grew up in the socialist system and liked it, I have nothing against that. If you talk to people in Bosnia & Herzegovina they will all tell you living in Yugoslavia was a dream compared to what happened to people afterwards. So I don't have anything against that system; but it's like they haven't left their slow red tape system behind completely and they haven't really embraced the more Western ways. So they are somewhere in between, and they are very slow moving, so therefore if you really want things to be done quickly, especially for the smaller organisations, the most effective way to help, I personally think its through local communities and local groups directly, and avoid red tape as much as possible.

I think also when you work with local groups and local communities, obviously they learn a lot from you and maybe you don't have to train them officially. I don't bring all these groups I am working with in Bosnia & Herzegovina in one room and I don't have a course for them, but I know I taught them the ways of doing things, so it can spread back. So in a way its capacity building just even cooperating with people like that, because they can show you and they can tell you how things work in Bosnia & Herzegovina the easiest way, the most direct way. But then again they learn so much from you as regards the paperwork and the accountancy and being accountable for where money is going, where it has come from.

Svenn: Always work with local partners. We don't see any need for us being onsite twenty-four/seven. When you have the experience we have now – I've now been doing this since '78 – the international community have spent so much money in the last twenty-thirty years, on education and capacity building. And I would say that in lots of these destinations we have very, very well educated people who are able to do what we are doing. So we would like local people to do more work. We think that is important – that people are able to do much of the development on their own. We are supervising, we have control over money, of course. But basically, we don't think it's needed for us to send people down to build a school when they have their local labour, and they have their architects, and they have their builders themselves that physically can do the job. And I think we've come so far now, the Western world, that we actually have to try and trust people. We give them facilities to build, and we help them in the process, but at the same time they have to get more and more responsibility.

And I think that's the right way to do it. So we don't override all their decisions, and how they would like to do things. We're talking about religion, we're talking about culture, we're talking about how things are usually done in countries, and I think we have to let people get on with their lives. So now we're supporting instead of dictating them how to do things. Of course, we may have to supervise sometimes, and sometimes we are supervised ourselves, and I think that's a very good way to do things. That we move together with communities, be with the community, and let the community do as much themselves as they can. But they need the security; they know that we are with them, so if there is a problem they can seek support.

Tajma: Often people are obsessed by doing things in a politically correct way. There are obviously different opinions about delivering aid and different opinions about the impact on the local economy. But take, for example, you have two elderly people living on thirty-three euros pension a month. Existing in Bosnia & Herzegovina is more expensive than in Ireland. The prices of coffee and sugar and everything else is the same as in Ireland. Now, you think two people can live on thirty-three euros a month? No they can't. Some of these people when they retired were doctors or accountants, and they used to have a good life, they used to have a normal life, going on holidays and driving cars, and now they are in old age or they were wounded in the war as a soldier or even a civilian. I am all for helping Bosnia &

Herzegovina to get on their feet, but in the meantime you can't let people starve, of course you have to help them. These are the people who worked all their lives, they were not poor before.

These people don't have money to buy food. What's the difference if the local shops are stuffed with food? If people don't have money to buy, people are equally hungry. I mean, obviously economic development of the country is hugely important, and the whole region, but if I said, 'There is a large group of people who don't have money to go to the shops to support local economy' – what do we do with them?

Also, it depends on the NGO and their control over aid. I remember when we were setting up a project, a student's support programme, we had all of these conditions attached to it. We find families who don't have any people or members of their family abroad. When we were setting out this programme, we really took the time to prepare and do the research and to check on people's backgrounds, so we make sure that people who are accessing our programmes don't have people abroad who can help them. I always say I have family in Bosnia & Herzegovina, my extended family is still there, but I always feel responsible for my family there and to help them myself, rather than put them on Cradle's list, and I expect that from other people as well.

We are NGOs – we are not supposed to think like government organisations. We are supposed to look at people, of course yes, we aresupposed to look at the big picture and be a part of the big picture, but I think if you are only looking at the big picture, then you are overlooking ordinary people who do need help at that particular moment. These people are like elderly and they are vulnerable. They won't survive by the time we get Bosnia and Albania and Moldova up and running as economically sound countries. They wouldn't survive it by then.

What I have learned, apart from everything else, is that working with people and talking with people and cooperating with people in the local communities is for me number one. The second thing is that we, the charities here in Ireland, should really share and should not be afraid of sharing even how we fundraise, where we get the money, because really, it is nearly like a competition I'm afraid to say. Everyone is afraid to say where they get the money and how they get it in case somebody else is trying to get the same or whatever. This is totally the wrong approach and I think we should cooperate more in Ireland amongst ourselves.

'Long term improvements need a long term plan'

–Moya McCann & Michael Gannon

Moya has a background in nursing and together with her husband Jack, a recently retired plastic surgeon from Galway University Hospital, set up **Irish Friends of Albania** in 2005 to help support the plastic surgery department of the Mother Teresa Hospital in Tirana, Albania. Michael (42) works as Project Coordinator for the charity in Galway.

> ❝ For me anyway, the key thing about something like this is, you need to have the three to five year plan ... One year is very short, and so you need the security a good funding campaign, whether you have it locally or you know you have to raise 'X' amount a year. It just means that you plan more steps ahead, with your volunteers and funders. ❞ *Michael Gannon*

Moya: The first contact with Albania for myself and my husband Jack was about eight years ago, in 2002. Jack is a plastic surgeon in the University Hospital in Galway. There was a little girl in a hospital in Albania, her name was Alba, she was very badly burned. One of Jack's junior doctors who had worked with him was doing some voluntary work over there. So he contacted Jack and asked would he be able to accept her for care in Galway. And the little girl came here, only four years old, very badly burned, she came over with her mother. Michael was living in Albania at the time, and he escorted them ... It was a huge culture shock for them, they hadn't a word of English and were from a fairly poor farming background, and they must have been terrified, coming out on three flights to a strange country, and worrying about the little girl's health.

And she stayed about four and a half months. She became a fixture down in the paediatric ward, everyone loved her. They got to know her. She went home healed. So they were coming in dribs and drabs with their parents, there again no English, huge culture shock to them. Most of them would require further follow up surgery so Jack felt, maybe if we go there – these are very severe deformities that we're seeing, so there might be a lot more people needing help. Michael was still living in Albania so we arranged with Michael to meet him over there and to meet the professor of plastic surgery. So we went to Albania in December '04 and by February '05 we had officially formed a charity.

We were based in the hospital that the little girl came from; it's called Mother Theresa Hospital in Tirana. In our December meeting we met with the professor of plastic surgery, and obviously, Jack being a plastic surgeon and he had plastic surgery colleagues, that was the logical direction to take, so that's where we based ourselves – in the plastic surgery unit.

So we went through the formalities, and we had our first trip with sixteen volunteers who went over in April of '05 for two weeks. Two weeks of very, very intensive work. These volunteers were doctors, nurses, a sterilisation expert and a bio-engineer. The idea all along has been to improve the skills of the local staff and make them as independent as possible, to pick up the things they'll be able to do for themselves. We have a commitment and promised to the doctors over there that they would observe, and scrub in and assist, and then do the operations themselves. And the same with the nurses. The nurses were reluctant at first to get involved, and there were a couple who were more inclined to come forward than the others – obviously, the more experienced girls and those with better English.

And they held clinics and the people were queuing up outside the clinic from five in the morning waiting to be seen, hoping to be seen. There were huge, huge numbers of people seen, and it was a long day working from about eight in the morning to about eight, nine, ten, eleven at night. They came from far and wide; they would have walked for hours down the mountain to get to the bus to bring them to the city and then start queuing up at the outpatient centre. It was a blind faith I think they had, in that there was a medical team waiting to see them.

Certainly I feel the skills are improving and the enthusiasm to learn is there. Also, as well as working with them in Albania, we've brought some of them to Ireland. We've brought about fifteen doctors and nurses to observe, but only to observe, unfortunately. The doctors would not be allowed to treat patients here in Ireland or to even scrub in the operations. They'd just purely observe, because of the medical registration, which is fair enough. And the same with the nurses. And then, because so many of the Irish doctors have been to the hospitals in Albania, they know what it's about, they're willing to take these people under their wing for the few days or the week, fortnight or whatever length of time that they're here. It's a commitment, but it's not a burden.

Michael: The thing for us really is that there were a few big moments. The foundation of the organisation was really due to a number of things coming together, as Moya said. The first contacts with Albania were around treatments for children. The first project that was set forward was really to see if we could change the way of working to actually bring surgical teams to Albania to see patients in clinic and treat them. So the team went and that was a big success.

From the spring of 2005 the charity was set up and the aim, as listed in its statute, was to bring aid by way of medical assistance to Albania. Fundraising started, and specific planning for a three-year programme of work. That was necessary, because long-term improvements of surgical staff and surgical facilities and everything related to that needed a long-term programme.

The early work involved seeing many patients in clinics and doing many operations. That has changed over the past couple of years for a variety of reasons. Some of them are budgetary and some of them were in response to what the local Albanian staff want themselves. In the departments where we are most active we now focus on teaching the Albanian personnel the more advanced procedures that they wish to learn. Over the course of a few visits, the Albanian staff progress from observing and assisting in the procedures to actually performing the operations themselves.

Both the Irish surgeons and Albanian surgeons are very busy – it's difficult to find enough time to plan things as well as possible. Teleconferencing is a big help. When we're physically in Albania there's a work pressure there, and in particular the Irish want to do work as much as possible, and get as many operations done as possible. Preparation for the visit and review of the visit

Staff at Mother Theresa Hospital in Tirana, Albania with Irish colleagues.
Photo: Irish Friends of Albania.

are very important as during the actual visit the work is intensive.

For me anyway, the key thing about something like this is, you need to have the three to five year plan ... One year is very short, and so you need that security for a good funding campaign, whether you have it locally or you know you have to raise 'X' amount a year. It just means that you plan more steps ahead, with your volunteers and funders. It's not that we'd be looking for a huge amount, but the comfort of knowing it's going to be there in two, three, four years time, so that you can hopefully map out a reasonable programme out of it.

My own personal opinion might be, from looking back over the years, from the point of view of advice and teaching and giving the people the benefit of experience of the Irish medical staff, I would love if it was at a point where their imparting of their own experience and their training for the Albanians was 50 to 60 per cent medical and technical, diagnosing the patient and recommending a procedure or treatment; and maybe 30 to 40 per cent organisational, and this is how we would run a hospital or this is how we would structure this service so that you can treat more patients and so that you can have a better working environment. You know, this is the management of a big hospital ... like anything, you train to be a surgeon or you train to be an actuary or an astronaut or whatever, and at the end of the day you still find yourself spending 30, 40 per cent of your time trying to sort the environment so that you can actually work. So that you can do the work, you have to have teamwork and you have to have budgets and you have to have a system.

Our next project actually includes our experts advising in the set-up and running of the new trauma centre at the hospital which is about to be finished. That would be a new departure, because potentially you have the opportunity to say to people, well listen, here's the big picture: how many staff do you have, how many this, how many that. Here's a template to run it. Here are the gaps. The idea of helping to plan for a trauma from the start. So we'll be able to recruit an expert – probably best an external one, because then they're free from politics in a lot of things – to get it set up and get it going. It's basically getting people to work together and giving them the space to work and having the sort of communication backup and bit of financial backup to make sure that it can work.

With our work, there's a huge amount of investment in people. It's the investment in people and programmes where you know people are trained up; some might be working in a government department who have been assisted or trained by that project and who really put the benefit of that to work. Unfortunately, though, some of it doesn't get carried on for years to come, because people emigrate or they go to another job. The successful projects and successful programmes are the ones where you have a staff or partners that you can stand over.

That requires a huge amount of communication – people just talking to each other quite a lot and understanding each other. It was very important in our small project here that a sizeable number of Albanian hospital personnel came to train in Ireland – fifteen over the years – because once people come in, you get up to a better level of communication with them, because they feel they know you, they feel they understand you a bit better and the relationship isn't so one-sided. I think those investments are worth it, once they're properly planned visits where they do productive things when they're here, and are expected to show the return on that. Just simply having the opportunity to have regular, real, working contact with European colleagues is a huge step forward, especially for the younger doctors and nurses.

One of the things that we've always tried to work on to a degree was to assist the local Albanian doctors and nurses to develop their professional groups at a national level. In surgery and medicine and nursing, your association and your peer group has a huge role to play in defining the standards. So, in other words, a plastic surgeon in Albania should be looking to his peer colleagues, you know, to be looking for guidance from them. Trying to involve them, to get to become full members of those peer groups, to give papers at conferences, to try and get the standards from them. So if it's a particular type of operation, how should it be done, what materials should be used, what protocols would be used, because that's ultimately how they can effect improvements, improvements in standards and improvements in quality by factually saying, well, this is what your peer association says is the norm or the standard for this.

I don't know if it's any different in Albania than in other countries as to how you can be effective and work effectively. Maybe as a paid worker, and someone who has been involved full-time I'm a lot more sensitive to the gaps. If I look at myself where I'm a volunteer ... I want to know things once a year or maybe once a month, and I give my input and I see improvements from one month to the next. I go away quite happy. And maybe I am blissfully unaware of a lot of commotion behind the scenes. And maybe that's the way that should be, too, for people who are involved as volunteers. Because if you're a volunteer you have your own job to do and your own interests, and you commit some of your free time to teaching a fellow surgeon in Albania or operating on a child or whatever, and maybe that's enough to ask of that person to do that.

'Change the hearts and minds of the administration'

–Debbie Deegan

Debbie (47) adopted seven-year-old Zena from Russia in 1998 and set up **To Russia With Love** shortly after to help care for the children in Hortolova orphanage where her daughter came from in Bryansk. To date, To Russia With Love has supported over 5,000 children living in State care.

> I would say one of the key things about our organisation is we actually work with the local governors and the local administrators instead of saying, 'We know better than you,' which really most people do. People from the West go in with the attitude: 'Look how fabulous we are, we know exactly how to do it, we're fabulous doctors, we're fabulous systems people, we're religious, we're this, we're that', and they're condescending.

We took two children on a holiday from Chernobyl, and when the one of them got into the car with us the night we collected them from the airport, on a very personal level she connected with us straightaway as a child. I said to my husband that night, 'I'm not going to send them back to the orphanage, I'm going to keep them illegally', which I did, but one of them had to go back, and the Health Board obviously wanted me to return both, because I wasn't qualified to adopt a child. I called over to the Russian Embassy, and they told me that they would allow Zena to stay with no paperwork on the

Misha, Vika, Tanya and Slava, who grew up in Hortolova orphanage in Bryansk region of Russia and progressed to study IT, Cardiac Surgery, Business and Law respectively at third level. (2008). *Photo: Dave Conachy / To Russia With Love.*

condition that they could call to my house any time unannounced, from the Embassy, and check our home or her school or her doctor. So I agreed to this and we kept her with no paperwork. So she was here for four years before we adopted her.

So in that period of time she started to speak English. She was seven when we took her and literally she'd no language other than we had a combined body language of mother-daughter, so when she started to speak she started telling about all the children she'd left behind. I was quite stunned and shocked that I hadn't considered her seven years previous other than I had this sort of grey image of an orphanage somewhere. So I went into Russia to find the children that she was telling me about, because she was very broken hearted at leaving some of them behind, and that was my first journey into Russia – I went in and it took me a while to find the orphanage she was from.

So I found this orphanage and it was a complete and utter sh**hole at the time. It was 1998, and Russia was on its knees, broken glass in the windows, minus thirty, no heating, no working toilets, and all Zena's classmates were there, who were all seven and eight as well. I made the commitment to the kids that I would try and change their lives. I came back to Ireland after my first visit, set up the charity, got a very strong board around me. I hadn't a clue how to run a charity, but I knew how to attract very good people and I'd brilliant people around me and I brought in brilliant managers, systems people.

I knew what I wanted, but I didn't have any of the skills, so I brought in people who had all the skills and I managed a team of people over the past twelve years that have had much better skills than me and I sucked all their information out of them. I landed all that information in Russia.

I would say one of the key things about our organisation is we actually work with the local governors and the local administrators instead of saying, 'We know better than you,' which really most people do. People from the West go in with the attitude: 'Look how fabulous we are, we know exactly how to do it, we're fabulous doctors, we're fabulous systems people, we're religious, we're this, we're that', and they're condescending. We would never condescend and we went in with the locals and we worked with them to make the changes. I mean, there are many social workers in Ireland that are driving round with kids in the back of their car and they don't know where to bring them. We're a country that's had twelve years of economic boom and we still can't get it right, you know. Our childcare system is a disgrace here. I was in Russia when the Murphy report broke. It was on every news bulletin in Russia, and I'm sitting in Russia telling them how to run their orphanages, and we had our own children here for decades in orphanages, ruining them, destroying them, raping them. Yet the Russians were wonderful about it, because I was upset about it, ashamed to be Irish, absolutely, listening to the reports coming out about our own orphanages, and there we are pontificating about how to run theirs, you know?

Really all our systems were based on what we perceived to be good parenting and what we'd do for our own, and if I was doing it for my own – I wouldn't shave my child's head, and I would give her a birthday party. So what we did was, we took a bunch of very sad, miserable, lonely children with low self esteem that were learning poorly and playing sports at a very low level. We put in layers and layers, from the smallest thing to the biggest thing. We put in big education programmes, but we also put in footballs and basketballs and football pitches, so they got everything that normal family children were used to getting and within about six or seven years we started seeing normal family children appearing.

My first ten years I had the same team of people and we based everything really on the fact that if that's what we do for our own, that's what we're going to do for them. So people would say, 'But he's only an orphan, why would you spend a thousand euro on a pair of skis for him?' Because I'd spend a thousand euro on my son's skis, so my children in Russia were skiing initially on wooden planks, and now some of them are skiing internationally. If you needed one-thousand-euro skis, you got them. If you needed train tracks on your teeth, you got it, if you needed a heart operation we brought you to Moscow for it, if you needed to find your mother, we find your mother. If you needed to be reunited with your siblings, that's exactly what we did.

When we first started, there was one little gold cup in the orphanage on a shelf, and I joke you not, now we have walls and walls and walls of, you know, those big cups with pillars and marble, and the kids all know that they're better than anybody else at any of the sports – our girls win ice skating competitions, our boys win football. We literally just poured as much as we could of what we knew was best of Ireland. I don't want to sound cheesy, but we brought in TLC on a grand scale, and it was the first time people had seen orphaned children be treated as proper human beings, not just give them an old coat or give them better porridge or give them Calpol or a furry toy from Ireland, or a broken computer off the back of a convoy. People will send out their crap and think they're great, getting rid of all their old broken toys, people used to give us jigsaws in the beginning with bits missing, because it was going to an orphanage. 'They should be grateful.' Why should they be grateful if there's bits missing of the jigsaw? I wouldn't be grateful if somebody gave me a jigsaw and there was bits missing, so we didn't allow any of that to happen for our children. We put them on the same level as family children and we gave them back their self-esteem.

Our children actually had opinions and began to use them and could make choices between jam or honey. You might think it's a small thing whether you want jam or honey, and it is a small thing, but when you get to seventeen or eighteen you can't make a choice about whether you want to be a prostitute or not. You do exactly as you're told; whereas from a very young age we started ours on, 'Do you want jam or honey, do you want those boots or these boots, do you want that coat or this coat?' Not because the coat mattered, but because we were teaching them how to make choices. A million different things chipped away at our children's self-esteem. In their own head, they weren't as good as family children, in their own head they couldn't dress like family children. We started adding and adding until we grew what I would consider to be a normal child.

The biggest thing we did in twelve years was change the self-esteem completely of the children, and we changed the hearts and minds of the administration we were working with, because twelve years ago orphans were these scabby things that lived out in a forest that really nobody wanted to look at or see or fund. And because consistently for years they saw us holding their hands, minding them, tucking them in at night … You know, when I rebuilt the first orphanage physically, the builders came in with sh** tiles, sh** toilets, cheap taps, and I said, 'No.' Our tiles were pink with roses on them; instead of being like basic six-inch white tiles that all orphans got all over Russia, we had beautiful pink tiles with roses on them, and the builders would say, 'Why would you bother picking tiles with roses on them? They're only orphans.' I'd say, 'Exactly that reason', so we lifted the spec up completely of everything. The governor made a pact with me after four years. I was still redoing my first orphanage and we were still ploughing through it, and the governor said to me, 'I'll have ten done by the time you're finished', and I said, 'I'll take on your challenge', and he renovated ten while I renovated one.

So two things we did: we changed the hearts and minds of the people and made them feel orphans were worthwhile; and we changed the level of self-esteem of the children. And once children felt that they were normal, then they felt they could go to college and universities and could actually mix with normal family children. They saw the improvement and the children, and then they saw that we were actually putting children into universities and colleges, and they actually couldn't believe that an orphan could become a doctor, it's not possible. We've a boy now who qualified last May to be a lawyer and people can't believe a lawyer could come out of an orphanage, you know, so the parties sat up and took notice.

Looking back, it took a decade to turn it round. I mean, I travelled 200 times to Russia in the first ten years and I took different people out with me on different trips, foster care experts, systems experts, hygiene experts, nutrition experts, management, civil servants, people who knew how to turn the system round. Because I had no time to speak to civil servants, they drove me mad, but I'm working in a civil service environment out there, so I had to stop saying, 'Actually I want to change this system and I need it done on Monday.' It could take Monday in two years' time before it was changed and that drove me nuts. I had to learn to work within their system instead of trying to implement our wonderful Western ways on them.

I think we're a very personal organisation, we know all the children incredibly well, and they're like our own children. The downside to that is that it's impossible to have a strategy to get out of it and to go back to a normal life, because the children look on us as their minders and their guardians and they don't have anybody else, so they know we have their back. I think that I made a personal commitment to a bunch of kids; I made a promise to them and I felt that every other person in their life had let them down and I just felt I wasn't going to let them down. And I haven't let them down yet. It's a huge responsibility, because now that there's no money in the economy here, how do I keep doing that for them? At the same time, the upside is that, because they feel they have guardian angels here in Ireland and we will put them through college, they've turned into doctors and lawyers. So the downside is the weight of responsibility I feel on our shoulders to try and sustain that, but the upside is we've doctors and lawyers.

The success grew more success. I wasn't anticipating twelve years ago to have 5,000 children under our wings. I had 200 kids in the beginning and my arms were full of those 200, and because it was so successful, 200 turned into 2,000 and then 5,000. I didn't anticipate that. It wasn't in the plan. Every time I look around there's a new class sitting behind me. My last visit in, I went into an orphanage and there was a whole class of little fellows, and one of those was sobbing his eyes out crying. They all cry for about a month initially, because it's a new environment, a horrible environment to come into, and he was absolutely sobbing, and I said to somebody, 'Don't even tell me his name', and that's the first time I've ever done that. I don't even want to know his name, because once you connect, that's it then, when he's fourteen I'll be still there, and when he's twenty-two I'll be still there, and I'm forty-seven, I'm doing this for twelve years and you just think, how long more can you just keep connecting with four-year-olds? And I just – it's an awful thing to say, but I just said, 'Don't tell me, I don't want to know his story, don't tell me his story.'

We've become parents to a huge amount of children and that's a massive burden. I've opened an office in Moscow called Children With Love recently and I'm trying to tap into Russian money, but it's a very, very difficult environment. I'm going to make them feel guilty about the fact that the small Irish shoulders have been carrying this burden and we can't – I feel my shoulders can't carry it for the next ten years. I need some Russian to come in and feel like he's going to be my saviour and take over the burden of it, if I can find that person.

'Think objectively'
–Joe McGrath

Joe (55) is a marketing lecturer in Dublin. He set up **Student Aid Chernobyl** in 2000 to bring third level students to Belarus and support local organisations through partnership and funding. Since then the organisation has brought 2,000 students to Belarus to engage in humanitarian activities.

> 66 I think the questions need to be asked. I think you need people to say, 'Detach yourself – get objective.' It's very hard to do, because people are passionate about this country. I think a lot of the reasons Irish charities are so long in Belarus would be this personal attachment, you know, the emotional attachment rather than the objectivity of saying – 'Right, these people will survive without us and thrive without us.' And the Belarusians, at the end of the day, are going to be responsible for Belarusians; not Irish people responsible for Belarusians. 99

Literally I got involved through, well, serendipity; I happened to be at the airport and waiting in Arrivals. I saw these kids coming in for – I think it was actually for medical care. So it wasn't any particular attachment to Belarus or anything particular about Chernobyl that rattled me in any way. It just happened to be a day at the airport; I saw very ill kids and I couldn't get it out of my head. As literally as serendipity, just that. I went out with a group months later, and I would have been involved in taking students abroad anyway before that, because I was very involved in sports at Dublin Institute of

Technology, and so the idea of getting students to do something useful in Belarus and taking them abroad was there.

I spent three years having an apprenticeship in Belarus – three years before I felt I'd learned enough to start thinking objectively, getting comfortable enough to say, 'Okay, what are we about?' To actually get enough knowledge of institutional care, state care, the economics, the culture, how people behave differently and so on. To get to that distance where you can make decisions based on the right thing to do rather than the emotional thing to do; the emotional, humanitarian response.

I can say we spent an awful lot of money, you know, chucking resources, chucking money at projects all over the place. All good stuff, but without a sense of a long-term strategy, and I think, in the end, the most important thing was having established a sense of ... a beginning, of knowing what you're doing. Spending, I think hundreds of hours talking and thinking about values. What are we about and what are our values in this and what are we doing here and all that. Now, that sounds very pious, but actually it is the most useful thing we've ever done, and I can literally remember it was hundreds of hours developing – a sense of mission.

I can remember the conversation where I asked, 'Well how do you make Sasha's life or Valentina's or Inna's life better? They're in an institution, what would be an ideal outcome for them?' And then we started thinking, 'Let's ask Sasha and Inna and Valentina, and let's ask their carers, let's ask the director of the orphanage', and that took months, maybe even years. 'Okay, I'm going to start listening to people?' And that was a huge sort of insight. Actually listen to the locals, listen to the people you're trying to help. Listen to directors of orphanages, to carers and so on.

I think every organisation has its own mission, whether it is articulated or not. Ours is very clear, it's to get young people out of institutions. Now, that's very, very simple, but we have to focus on that. Otherwise you're going to end up doing forty good things, but they're unfocused. I don't think the mission ever embraced, 'Let's get every kid out of every institution', because we haven't. I doubt we ever could, we're not big enough, but also, that's a Belarusian job, a Belarusian task.

We built a house and we administer it with the Department of Social Protection, a house for kids that formerly lived in institutional care, so I would have known these kids ten years ago. So okay, they have to live with, if you like, physical or mental disabilities, but some were capable of independent living; so we showed them a house in the suburbs about forty kilometres away from the institution and said, 'If you would like to live there, you will learn how to be independent, you'll learn to cook, you'll learn to go shopping, you'll learn to buy a bus ticket, get a job.' And it's worked.

Now, we can only do that with the cooperation of the local Ministry of Social Protection, and we have that, and the deal was we'd pay for – because this is a new concept in Belarus – we'd pay for the salaries of five housemothers and all the costs of the house. Then we got this idea of getting people out of institutional care where we can. That's worked, and I guess if I was to say, okay, after ten years, you know, one of the things I'm happiest with, it is that concept of where people can move out of institutional care, we've begun that process. Now, that meant working very, very closely with Ministries, you can't just do these things without high levels of engagement with local people.

We have to make decisions around who owns it, you know. Who has got ownership of that? The Belarusians. I had to really work this out, because I knew that we're not going to be there twenty-four hours a day and there will be problems. I mean, there's huge problems when you start getting people deinstitutionalised. But they are problems that can be solved locally, not from Dublin. So we had to let go and hope that everything goes well and it has.

So much so that they asked us at a much more senior level in the Ministry, could we do it again, but would we, if you like, work very closely with their senior people in establishing a new place? So right now we've more or less put the money together to do it. We're building a place, again it's a home. It will be home to about eight young people. It will take us two years to build and when it's built it will be the first opportunity for a particular region to have a place where people that would be institutionalised for the rest of their lives will learn how to live independently.

And they're homes, they're not mini-institutions, you know, that's one of the things we have to try to persuade the Belarusians to think about. They would say, 'Why don't you move twelve people in, or twenty?' And I say, 'No. Home, a family, is generally around six, seven, eight people.' There will be a housemother. They will get to know the local community – we always put them in villages, you know. The idea is that when this is rolled out by the government, always in a village or a suburb, it's got to be part of the community. So we're working right now with the community. We've got the community involved

Aleksander Lomaia, Georgian Minister for Education and Science, and Mary Robinson, Former President of Ireland, at a round table discussion on child welfare and de-institutionalisation in Tbilisi (October 2006). *Photo: First Step Georgia.*

in building this house. We will be, over the next few months, getting our Belarusian partners to have meetings with the local community.

The type of dialogue with the community will be: okay, you've never seen people with disabilities, because traditionally they're locked away, so we'll introduce you to people with some disabilities and get them to talk about life. So, involving the community from day one so that they're not calling this house the mental house or whatever the Belarusian equivalent is.

Now rather stupidly, I think, we agreed to pay for the staff for the place in Rechitca for three years too many. It's a big draw on our resources. I know we'll be asked to fund salaries when we build this new place, it's called Tereshkovichi, and I'm going to say, 'No.' I'm going to say, 'We've done our bit.' We've invested something like 80,000 euro when this thing is finally built, and I think we're telling the state: 'Listen, you guys find the money. You're getting wealthier, find the money. It's five salaries.'

And not everybody is capable of independent living and that's a harsh reality, you know. There are people in Ireland that we put away in institutions, and we call them mental health hospitals and all of that. We don't use the word asylums anymore, but you know, they're pretty much the same. People that we effectively take out of society for their own protection or for the protection of society, we do it in all countries, you know. In some ways we just do it more benignly, because we know better and because the press scrutinises and all that. In Belarus I think that's beginning to happen.

It's not just about building a place, it's working with the Belarusians to say, 'Okay, this is the process that we both go through, we both learn from, so that you can recreate that in every region in Belarus.' And that's the mission if you like. It's not really about building; it's about the knowhow, the knowledge, and when they have that, there's no need for us anymore.

So it's been ten years, but right now I am genuinely thinking I've never felt the way I have for the last year or so, which is, you know, we're getting near the end game here. We're getting near mission accomplished. Let's start looking at end game activities. Let's ask the impertinent and unpopular question, 'What is the end game?'

You've got to get very objective about Belarus, and start calling it Belarus and not Chernobyl. You just look at it as a country and see it is right in the centre of Europe, it's friendly with the CIS states and it is moving, if you like, at least looking towards the European Union. Economically the country is making great progress, growth rates are 6 to 8 per cent and have been very consistent. Basically, Belarus is economically moving in the right direction. The answer then to all the social problems, the ones of institutional care, orphanages and all the rest of it, is the government is richer, and has the money to spend.

All those stories you hear that Belarusians are cruel, it's wrong. They care about their kids, they care about their disabled, they care about their orphans and it's been lack of resources. And I feel certain to say I think lack of knowledge has also been the problem – like what are the standards in these areas? So increasingly they are becoming economically more well off, and they also have the knowledge to address problems. There will be always small pockets where institutional care is not good and where state care is not good, but they're increasingly smaller pockets, and I trust the Belarusians to, as they get more wealthy, take care of those pockets.

The Belarusians would much prefer that Irish, Italian, English charities spent their money in Belarus. They've said, 'Listen, we do have institutions, we'd like to make these institutions better.' Okay, and they're right. And the resources we spend taking kids out of Belarus in the summer months could be spent on these institutions. And Irish people have seen this, but you know, we're used to having these little kids in and it's great fun and you know, it makes us all feel good, but actually, they're right; Belarusians are right. Invest in making the state systems better.

When do we know the job in Belarus is finished? Forget about all the sentimentality that you've been working with people for five years, ten years, fifteen years, the same people. Of course people build attachments to those kids, to the same kids. It would be very hard for them at any level, but just at a normal human level, to say, 'I'm never going to see Evgenya again …' But that needn't necessarily be so. They can take Evgenya anytime they want on a holiday, but you know, it's Evgenya on a holiday, not Evgenya adding two years to her life, just because she spent a month or two in Ireland. And if that money was there to make Evgenya' s life great or better eleven months of the year instead of one month a year, I think it would be better spent in Belarus.

I think the questions need to be asked. I think you need people to say, 'Detach yourself – get objective.' It's very hard to do, because people are passionate about this country. I think a lot of the reasons Irish charities are so long in Belarus would be this personal attachment, you know, the emotional attachment rather than the objectivity of saying – 'Right, these people will survive without us and thrive without us.' And the Belarusians, at the end of the day, are going to be responsible for Belarusians; not Irish people responsible for Belarusians. Yeah, it's going to be hard though; if I ever leave Belarus, and I will at some stage, there'll be a huge number of friends and relationships that I'll be leaving behind, and that's after an investment of ten years.

Because to deliver, going back to values, to do it right, to absolutely be singing off the same hymn sheet really, reading from the same script, takes time. It takes a huge investment in time, because you cannot work with people where there isn't a shared vision of the future. But if you spend the time, then things happen, you know, and they happen to a plan and everybody knows everybody's point of view and their concerns and their ambitions and all that sort of thing. That takes just so much time, but I think you have to do it. You're going to be a good listener. You're going to be a good communicator. You're going to, you know, not run everything to your own priorities, but to consider the priorities of others while still maintaining a sense of your own mission.

I think small works. Smaller organisations build the relationships; they get to know the community, the orphanage, the institution; even the local nurses and doctors. So, yeah, I think the small organisations work. It does require time to do the negotiation and build the relationships, and it doesn't happen overnight, and then you get back again to this. To build a relationship, it's more individuals and small teams that tend to make the breakthroughs.

'Stop before you intervene'
–Fiona Dowling

Fiona (38) volunteered in an orphanage in Romania with **Comber – for a future without orphanages** (formerly Comber Romanian Orphanage Appeal) as a physiotherapist in 1994 for six months. She subsequently stayed involved with the organisation and became Comber's executive director in 2006. Comber works with children and adults with disabilities in Giurgiu County.

> **That probably in some ways was the biggest turning point for me, that real realisation of asking people at every level what they need before you go in. Stopping before you intervene. Just to take a pause and see what the situation is and find out what might be needed instead of ... instead of arriving at the door of the orphanage and thinking everyone needs clothes, which obviously they do. But pausing to see why they don't have clothes.**

I do remember December 1989 and the fall of Ceausescu – I would have been in my final year of school. So I remember that, and I remember a lot of coverage around the fall of communism. But it would have been two years later before I really became aware of what was considered the scale of the problem for children living in orphanages in Romania – the reports that there were hundreds of thousands of children that had been placed in orphanages and the conditions were particularly bad for children with disabilities.

I mean, everyone says it who has worked in orphanages in Romania in the nineties: it was horrendous. Everything about the sights, the smells, the overcrowding, the kids clambering all over you ... It was heartbreaking. The first few days would still be in my mind as one of the most traumatic events of my life. And I do remember in the first week literally sitting in a coffee shop somewhere thinking, 'I'll have to go home, I won't be able to do it.' It was just so deeply disturbing. The level of neglect, I think, is still unimaginable. Supporting a child with a disability within a family setting is so totally and utterly different from supporting a child with a disability in an institution setting like that.

And then, because I was a new grad and although I had the basic skills, as time went on I definitely would say I was utterly overwhelmed by the amount in front of me. I remember walking around the first orphanage the first day and saying to my colleague, 'Where would you even begin?' And she was more practical than me and said, 'You start with one child', which has always stuck in my mind. But I was utterly overwhelmed by the fact that there was two of us covering four hundred children ... just overwhelmed by the volume of work.

But we really believed we were training the care staff and that we were really going to make a huge difference long term in the lives of the kids, so we felt very constructive and very productive. We had our routine timetable and we did do specific training programmes, so we would have taken groups of care staff and tried to really explain the basics of disability and try to explain the needs of the kids. Which looking back on it was so unbelievably naïve, because we had so little understanding of where the care staff were coming from. I remember being told that they work very long hours, the pay is very bad, they've never been trained, they're only working here because it's the only employment in the village. But I didn't really take that on board until years later, until I got to know them as people.

I suppose they were just at a place in their lives that was so far removed from where we were at. And we to them represented everything they couldn't have. We were waltzing in from Western Europe, we were wearing what we considered our oldest clothes and they were clothes they would never have had, you know, like Reebok runners, things that they'd never had access to in their lives. We just didn't build up the kind of relationship that would have made a difference with the staff. We in theory did all the right things, and we really invested massive time into training the staff, and we failed, without question. Because nothing was continued when we weren't there. Even on the weekends. I mean literally, we were there Monday to Friday and nothing was continued over the weekends. And if you happened to be there for some reason out of hours, you knew there was pretty much nothing going on that had been introduced when you were there.

I would have known the carers identified the kids who were mobile and bright as the priorities without question. And as a physio, and part of my personality, I would have had exactly the opposite opinion. I would have seen that the kids lying down being fed out of bottles are going to die, so they're a priority. So I would have thought exactly the opposite. Those children had a right to something totally different from what was available. That to me was black and white. So even if the carers didn't feel it was a priority to keep a child with severe disabilities alive, that to me was absolutely a contradiction to that child's human rights. So I did feel black and white about it, and a certain gut reaction part of me still does feel they have a right to something else, so nobody had a right to deny them that. I suppose I wanted the carers to be able to see that. I wanted them to see that this child has a right to sit in a chair, to interact with their environment, to get fed like a human being, to be spoken to.

More so than the kind of physio side of me wanting them to use the equipment, I wanted somehow to be able to believe or to facilitate that happening. I would still struggle with understanding the reason behind it. I know the system and everything and I know they were overworked, but that actual literally leaving a child who couldn't move sitting soaking and dirty all day long with flies all over them when there was a carer in the room or maybe having a coffee in the room beside it, I would still really struggle to understand that. And maybe I will sometime, I don't know. I have flashes of understanding parts of it, but I would still think I would find it really hard to know how you could stand by and watch that. My deepest personal connection with the kids I've worked with in Romania is that. They have nobody, especially the kids who have severe disability; they have nobody to speak out for them.

Over the next couple of years there was the whole move towards EU accession and the move towards deinstitutionalisation, the move towards closing orphanages, and that persuaded us at Comber that we could do a little bit more. So around 2004, 2005 we could see that children's orphanages

Residents of *Casa Comber* group home in Giurgiu County, Romania, enjoying a meal together. *Photo: Comber – for a future without orphanages.*

were closing and we started to track the closures. We started to look at where children were going, and then also we knew the children when they were over eighteen were moved into a different system, so we started to visit some of the institutions that those teenagers went to. Nobody seemed to be paying any attention to the fact that the children that all of us worked with in the '90s were actually being moved to adult versions of the same institution and nobody was paying any attention to it. And that kind of triggered us to make a decision to change focus and say that we were going to focus on over-eighteens.

I went onto the Comber board in 2000. By 2005 we had made a decision that we would try to see, would this work, and could we get one group home in the community for eight young people with disabilities who'd lived in institutions all their lives? And in 2006 I was asked then would I become essentially their first executive director for six months, on a trial period, to see could we get one group home up and running.

That's when I think it became very different for me, not just to do with it becoming my job, but I would say that period of really analysing things a bit more without the emotion – the really strong emotional reaction to everything I saw. I would still have moments of that, like when I visit an institution in Romania that is really substandard and get that kind of heartbreak and think, 'Oh God, there's still people living in these conditions.' But I would now say I have very little emotional, or much less emotional response to it. Partly because it's my job, but partly because I suppose I became a bit more analytical about it, or maybe we became more analytical in our approach.

So we essentially decided on a pilot basis to see could we support eight people with disabilities to move out of an institution into the community, and we opened Casa Comber in the beginning of 2007. And essentially huge changes happened for us then in that we really worked for twelve months in establishing some kind of relationship with the local county council, and we were tireless about it, because they were really, really, really not interested. And there was constant change of personnel; it was really a political system. It was a good time, though, because they were coming into the EU and people found it very difficult to say no at the time. Still, very, very little interest. I remember turning up at meetings and literally feeling like the directors here are just hiding under the desk. We were really, really persistent and tireless until we established, I wouldn't say we have a perfect partnership with the local government, but we have one that works and we've really persevered with that.

The most useful piece of advice I got at the time – we had the idea that we would open the home and fund the staff for a period of time to show the county council that it could be done, and a contact at the time absolutely said, 'Provide the capital funding; don't get involved in the ongoing funding of the homes.' And we took his advice and we waited a full twelve months until we had a signed commitment from the county council to say that they would fund the home after we opened it, and we have stuck with that for every new service that we've opened since. We've never opened it until we got a commitment from the county council that they'd cover ongoing costs. It delayed the project at least twelve months at the beginning, because we had to be so patient and persistent, but if we hadn't done that we'd still be on that one home that we'd be frantically trying to fund staff for. So that was a big change for us, it put the real focus on the capital funding and trying to engage local funding for ongoing costs.

Around that time I literally tried to find out everything that everyone was doing – in Romania and potentially related projects in other countries – and so I tried to go and meet with anyone I could get my hands on in Ireland that was doing similar work to see what they were doing. I looked at a lot of Irish disability service providers to see how they moved away from institutional care and what worked to be more integrated in community lives. I mean, I literally drove around the country and just travelled to see what was happening. Probably for me the biggest thing was having exposure to a variety of different organisations and types of practice to know what worked. I would feel that I learned slowly. And some of my huge learning has been from what has happened in Ireland, what has worked in Ireland, what is considered useful for an individual and what is considered good practice for an organisation.

The first group home blew us away, we just did not dream that it would work so well, I think. We chose eight people with minimal disability to move into the first home, because we needed it to work; so we chose people who we felt had very good potential to adapt to community living, because we needed the county council to see it's perfectly acceptable and reasonable and practical to support people to live in the community outside of an institution.

There's been also difficulties as we've opened more homes – we've struggled to keep the standard as high as it was in the first home and we'll have to redesign our system of mentoring and support in the homes. We haven't defined enough standards that we want in the homes or some of the operational procedures around them, and then there's the complication of the home being funded by us, the staff being funded by the county council – we don't have authority over the staff even though we have a system of mentoring and support.

And now I suppose we're at a point where we're looking at day services, employment services, a wider range of services, and we're also at a point now where we're going to try and focus even more on the quality of services we deliver. I suppose for the first couple of years after I took the job it was all about new things – funding for the next home, getting more people out, quite a focus on numbers. And we always approached funders with the fact that we have eight people out, we've got sixteen people out, whereas now I would say we're trying to look at a much broader picture around quality of life. We always knew it was more than getting people into a home, but to really look at the long-term futures of the people involved. So we're looking at not just the next step and the next home and the next capital project, but a wider look at the needs of people with disabilities and their services. And this is the really slow part …

So while we have staff in Romania, the strategic development and the funding and the project management is coming from Ireland, and the biggest change that needs to come for us is to really shift that over to Romania. We haven't worked on building local capacity enough. We've done training within the homes for staff. We have organised a number of exchange visits to Ireland; we've brought people over from the county council as well as people from the homes. So we have looked at capacity building in a general sense, but we haven't looked at developing an organisation that's going to be able to continue this work after Comber Ireland as such, and I think that needs to be our biggest change now.

Even though we're saying that services are less developed in Eastern Europe at the moment – I can see there's so many opportunities for change – but we really can learn from what exists already and we don't need to be going out in our droves to try and reinvent the wheel, which is essentially what I think we did try to do. And there's so much locally we could learn from that we weren't aware of or didn't take the time to be aware of. And my biggest advice is to look at everything that is there, because we haven't discovered the problem – we didn't uncover something. Like Columbus didn't discover America – it was there already. There's a system there already, if we were going to be able to support change we need to be able to do it from within, not outside, which I think is what we kind of tried to do.

I did some courses in international development that would have really helped me to understand. That approach of really asking people what they needed, I know it sounds so simple, I know I didn't know it when I went there the first time. That was a process of learning, definitely. And that probably, in some ways, was the biggest turning point for me, that real realisation of asking people at every level what they need before you go in. Stopping before you intervene. Just to take a pause and see what the situation is and find out what might be needed instead of … instead of arriving at the door of the orphanage and thinking everyone needs clothes, which obviously they do. But pausing to see why they don't have clothes. That was a real learning for me, that your gut reaction is the child is hungry I have to feed them; not saying that you don't have to feed a hungry child, but saying you need to know why they don't have food.

'Keep things small so you can handle them'

–Kieran Byrne, Pat Whelan & Fr Celsus Tierney

Kieran operates a haulage business in Wexford. He set up **Heart To Hand** in 1991 with his wife and since then has distributed hundreds of containers of aid and funding to projects in the Balkans, Asia and Africa. Pat (38) is a project manager from Tipperary and organises construction projects and volunteers for the charity. Fr Celsus (50) became involved in 1998 through organising food collections in his parish near Thurles.

> We do a lot of work with the Sisters, because we knew them and they were genuine and they were doing the right thing. We knew they were going to be distributed to the right people. There was nothing went astray. We wanted to keep it small. I like to keep things small so you can handle things. Small is beautiful, you can handle things on the ground, you know. It's not control I want. You know your lorries are going here and I always say, 'I know where they are going and I know that when they get there, they go off and they're safe.' *Kieran Byrne*

Kieran: We saw it on television in 1991, when Ceausescu was shot. It was the start of war. We said we'd do something for these children and we said we'd get together – my wife and myself – and that's really how we started. And we went out and started collecting money around the local farmers and

Sr Theresa Marie, Missionaries of Charity, at the opening of a new church and community centre in Ushtarak, Durres, Albania built by volunteers from Ireland (2010). *Photo: Heart To Hand.*

local neighbours and in one afternoon we went out for three hours and collected £5,500, so that was a start. I spent two weeks on the road going to every school in Wexford, and anywhere I could come across – I'd just call in looking for food, beans or anything we could get our hands on that time. That was the start of that, and the next thing the priest announced it off the altar that we was going to Romania. And we started on that and the next thing, the loads started coming in. Now, what do we want? We want baby food obviously, because the children obviously wanted food.

Where were we going with this? We hadn't a clue. So the next thing we do, friends of mine in Arklow, they said, 'You are going to Romania aren't you' and I said, 'Yeah, we're going.' They said, 'Where you going?' I said, 'We don't know where we are going really.' 'Well, somebody said you should go to Mother Teresa's Orphanage, they're the people.' So now I had to go look for Mother Teresa's Orphanage. I didn't know anything about Mother Teresa or her orphanage and I didn't know Mother Teresa either.

So now then people start bringing stuff into us, people just driving into our yard, dropping off maybe ten packages of nappies or people dropping baby food in. We didn't go look for it, they came and dropped everything.

Next thing our house became full. You couldn't get into bed at night, you'd be tripping over something, and this went on for six months. So I could only afford to send one truckload, so we got a lend of a truck from another crowd. And I got a couple of pallets, and I wasn't going to go at first, because I said, 'I'll send the drivers', and the next thing somebody said, 'It'll be sold on the black market.' So I said, 'I'd better go myself.'

And we had our address where we were to go in Romania. So when we arrived at the address where we were going, a children's orphanage, these nuns would take nothing from us, because they said, 'You must have stolen this, where would you get that kind of stuff?' We said, 'What do you want, Sister?' And she said, 'But you couldn't have this for free?' I said, 'Yes, free of charge from Ireland.' So she said, 'Have you any beds?' I said, 'How many do you want?' So we give her ten new single beds. I said, 'You want some sugar?' 'Oh sugar, yes.' So we gave them ten bags of sugar. So the nuns really came out, these are small Indian nuns. They unloaded the whole load.

And Mother Teresa was right then in Romania at the time, actually, and I met her and she said to me, would I bring aid to her Sisters in Albania or Warsaw? And I said, 'No Mother, we won't be here anymore, this is only a once-off.' And she took my hands and she squeezed them and she said, 'God will provide.' Whether that was a good day or bad day for me I don't know, we are still going after twenty years. So we named her, she's our patron of our charity, Mother Teresa. So this is how it all started. Then we went to other areas, then as the loads kept coming in we used to send loads into Romania for food and supplies and whatever they needed. I'd say, 'What do you want?' And they'd say, 'I want this, I want that and the other.' This was how we kept going.

And then we met volunteer after volunteer. Well, I had met with Father Celsus, because he collects food for us every year, and Pat got involved in the building, and we all came together as one group. And this is really where we got going. This is where we all are – I always say when people work for Heart to Hand, we all become members of their charity. You know, we're just one group, we're all voluntary, there's no money being passed here. I have my own business, Pat has his own, Father has his own, and this is the way we work and this is how it continues to work.

Pat: It's all about context and in finding the people. If I can't do what Kieran has asked me, my job is to find somebody who can, you know, or somebody who at least has the knowledge to help. We have volunteer teams go out to build in Albania now every year. The buildings that we are putting up at the moment act as a church mainly, and then they're used as community centres, they're used as a school. They're used as a meeting place and they can have their nativity plays there. Community centres, really. It draws the community together, and the feedback that we've had since we've started them has been phenomenal, that we've had to start building them bigger and bigger each year, because they're not able to hold the crowd that turns up. It is something new that the parish didn't have before.

The Missionaries of Charity organises it; they're on the ground every day, they know where the need of something like that is, so they organise the site and then they contact us and we take it from there. That's how it always works. And then they're run by the community; usually the caretaker would be somebody who is either living next door or living across the road or whatever, and he'd be in charge of the building and maintain it and keep it right and make sure there's nothing broke, it is not broken into.

We have moved recently to purchasing more materials in Albania than previously, because they're more accessible now, they stock more products close to what we're used to. So this year we've spent quite a lot of money out there buying all the building materials: windows, doors, insulated panels, floors, all that kind of stuff, which helps everybody locally out there and that in itself then encourages the locals to help you, because they see that you're spending money out there as well.

Kieran: We have a lot of nuns we work with; it's people we know. We do a lot of work with the Sisters, because we knew them and they were genuine and they were doing the right thing. We knew they were going to be distributed to the right people. There was nothing went astray. We wanted to keep it small. I like to keep things small so you can handle things. Small is beautiful, you can handle things on the ground, you know. It's not control I want. You know your lorries are going here and I always say, 'I know where they are going and I know that when they get there, they go off and they're safe.' I would be into feeding. I want to feed the poor; it's mostly soup kitchens we provide for.

We have different charities to look after. Each year we plan; like money will be needed there, to buy stuff there, and then that will be coming down the road. Coming up to Christmas, we have three trucks; we're thinking about sending three lorries out of food and supplies; two to Albania and one to Romania. So, we'll write to them to say, 'What do you want? Like what kind of food? What do you actually need?' And they'll say, 'I want ten tonne of flour, I want four tonne of sugar, I want a tonne of pasta, I want a tonne of rice', whatever it is. And these are groups that we have helped out down through the years; so we send them in what they want or as much as we can. Whatever they want.

Every year, this time of year, we'll be getting butter and cheese from local farmers, and they get a few pounds by selling jam on a Sunday outside churches, and this kind of thing. Little things, but little things are very important. We've old age pensioners saving five pound a week in Ireland like, this goes on. One puts five euro a week aside to buy tin meat for them and another one then would buy pasta out of old age pension like, you know, and all this kind of thing. We had an old man in Dublin here, and he did this for four or five years until he died, every few months he'd phone me up and say, 'When you coming up for the meat?' And you go out for the meat and there's holy pictures and all this. And he said, 'I'll have more for you next month now.' It'd bring a tear to your eye, that kind of thing you know, people helping people.

We go to schools and we try anything out this time of year. We try to get food in, because food is the big thing. Things are different – it's hard to keep raising money. I don't advertise or anything like that. I mean, there's people collecting for charities all over. Really and truly, I'd say 90 per cent of our money is in the providence of God, really. I would say anyway, because I don't know where the money comes from sometimes. I'm sure God will provide, I'm sure, if he wants us to go out. So this is my story.

Fr Celsus: It's a human story, isn't it? I suppose every time you hear a story like that, it kind of highlights the fact that in the face of all of the problems that people face, one person can make a difference. We oftentimes think, 'What little difference would my contribution make? It'll make no difference at all in the face of the environment or in the face of the economic problems or in the face of banking crisis or in the face of world hunger', or whatever; and one person can make a difference.

I suppose it is like the ripples in the water, that if one person does a little bit you'll never know who will be inspired or who might respond from that and take it on. All of us has gotten involved in various different ways, and I suppose you can tell your own story and how you got involved and who inspired you and what small little event it might have been; an insignificant event maybe, and you just said, 'I want to do something like that', and your life has changed. It has a different focus, you know … you're going in a different direction to where you thought you might be going.

We have made some fantastic friends over there over the years. Very good people who give their time to the cause. I think it's invaluable as well, the contacts that we make here at home. You know, we have a network at home now of people that would never come together; would never have any reason to come together. We're now best buddies kind of thing with various different professionals. And they're all part of the group now and they all have one focus and one kind of aim. It's not really the contacts we've made outside, it is the network that we have made at home. People are used to their own life, but to finally be a member of a charity, their own charity, I think, is unique in itself.

List of Interviewees

Herbert Armitage – Friends of the Children of Chernobyl (herbertarmitage@yahoo.co.uk)

Svenn Braamark – Cradle (www.cradle.ie)

*****Kim Boyle** – Romanian Challenge Appeal (www.romanian-challenge.org)

Kieran Byrne – Heart to Hand (www.hearttohand.net)

*****Marian Connelly** – Parents of Adopted Romanian Children (parcireland@eircom.net)

Stephen Conway –Team Hope (www.teamhope.ie)

Fiona Corcoran – Greater Chernobyl Cause (www.greaterchernobylcause.ie)

Audrey Cranston – Health Action Overseas (www.hao.ie)

Mairie Cregan – Aurelia Trust (www.aureliatrust.ie)

*****Mick Croghan** – Chernobyl Orphans Fund (www.chernobylorphansfund.org)

Henry Deane – Chernobyl Lifeline (henrydeane@me.com)

Noel Deane – Friends of the Children of Chernobyl (deane2@hotmail.co.uk)

Debbie Deegan – To Russia With Love (www.torussiawithlove.ie)

Fiona Dowling – Comber – for a future without orphanages (www.comber.ie)

Michael Gannon – Irish Friends of Albania (www.irishfriendsofalbania.com)

*****Carrie Garavan** – Comber – for a future without orphanages (www.comber.ie)

*****Trina Gilchriest** – Chernobyl Children International (www.chernobyl-international.com)

Liam Grant – Chernobyl Aid Ireland (www.chernobylaidireland.ie)

*****Frances Haworth** – Moldova Vision (www.moldova.ie)

Ned Hayden – Burren Chernobyl Project (www.burrenchernobyl.ie)

Conor Hughes – Cross Cause (www.crosscause.ie)

Tajma Kapic – Cradle (www.cradle.ie)

Patricia Keane – Rebuild for Bosnia (www.rebuildforbosnia.org)

Michael Kinsella – Ierlande-Moldova (www.ierlandemoldova.org)

Moya McCann – Irish Friends of Albania (www.irishfriendsofalbania.com)

Tom McEnaney – International Orphanage Development Programme (www.chernobyl.ie)

Joe McGrath – Student Aid Chernobyl (www.bike2belarus.com)

Caroline McGreal – Tanner Romanian Mission (www.tannerromaniamission.com)

Jim McQuaid – School Aid Romania (www.schoolaidromania.com)

John Mulligan – Focus on Romania (www.focusonromania.net)

Brian O'Sullivan – Burren Chernobyl Project (www.burrenchernobyl.ie)

*Easther Quinn – Belarus Ireland Adoption & Parents Society

Fr Celsus Tierney – Heart to Hand (www.hearttohand.net)

*Helen Walmsley – Voluntary Service International (www.vsi.ie)

Simon & Deena Walsh – Chernobyl Children's Trust (www.chernobylchildrenstrust.ie)

Pat Whelan – Heart to Hand (www.hearttohand.net)

Stephen Wilson – Adventist Development and Relief Agency (www.adra.ie)

Stuart Wilson – Zest4Kidz (www.zest4kidz.com)

*These interviews are available on the Network website – www.easterneurope.ie

Resource Directory

♣ = Irish-based organisation or website

The following resources are provided to enable those interested in learning more about the various themes discussed in this book the opportunity for further research. The directory includes resources on good practice in the fields of aid effectiveness, disability, children and community development, as well as organisational resources on areas such as managing volunteers, fundraising and governance. The directory lists some of the key Irish agencies and Codes of Good Practice supporting the not-for-profit sector, as well as a selection of useful international resources.

♣ Activelink (www.activelink.ie)
Hyperlink Ltd, Rear 6 Upper Grand Canal St, Dublin 4. T: (01) 6677326 / E: info@activelink.ie
The Activelink website provides information to the Irish non-profit sector on jobs, volunteering, forthcoming events, fundraising, training, publications and funding. The website is updated daily and produces two weekly newsletter bulletins: *Activelink*, which focuses on jobs and volunteering, and *Community Exchange*, which is dedicated to training and events.

Aid Workers Network (www.aidworkers.net)
A UK-based independent online community of over 10,000 international aid workers from around the world. The website contains practical information on working in the humanitarian and development sector, including 'how-to' guides, checklists, background briefings, aid workers' blogs, links to online resources recommended by peers, and a forum where aid workers can ask questions and swap tips. Members can sign up for the weekly email newsletter, *Aid Workers Exchange*.

BBC News Country Profiles
(www.news.bbc.co.uk – search term: country profiles)
Provides informative country overviews of various countries in Central and

Eastern Europe, giving a synopsis of a country's historical, political and economic background, as well as its key institutions. Some overviews include audio and video clips from the BBC archives.

Better Care Network Toolkit (www.bettercaretoolkit.org)
The Better Care Network Toolkit was developed in the U.S. to support practitioners and policy makers around the world in delivering better quality care for children who require an out-of-home placement. The toolkit contains a selection of downloadable guides and manuals, chosen as examples of good practice and for their global relevance, particularly for less-developed countries.

♣ **Boardmatch Ireland** (www.boardmatchireland.ie)
35 Exchequer St, Dublin 2. T: (01) 671 5005 / E: info@boardmatchireland.ie
A free web-based service that allows registered charities to recruit board members. Professionals from the private and public sectors register their interest in volunteering on non-profit boards and, based on their location, skills and preferred area of interest, are matched to available roles. Boardmatch also provides training for board members, aimed at improving governance standards of non-profit boards, and holds networking meetings for Chairs of charity organisations.

♣ **Carmichael Centre** (www.carmichaelcentre.ie)
North Brunswick Street, Dublin 7. T: (01) 873 5702 /
E: info@carmichaelcentre.ie
Carmichael Centre is a shared office and services facility for the not-for-profit sector. The Centre also provides training on topics such as charities legislation, governance and leadership, administration and planning, and human resources; as well as customised training and consultancy support. The Centre website contains an online library, with good practice guides and 'how to' factsheets on a range of topics.

Centre for Global Development (CGD) (www.cgdev.org)
CGD is an independent, non-profit policy research organisation, dedicated to reducing global poverty and inequality. CGD conducts research and analysis on a wide range of topics related to how the policies of wealthy countries impact the developing world, including aid effectiveness, education,

globalisation, health, migration and trade. The CGD Commitment to Development Index quantifies the full spectrum of rich country policies that have an impact on increasing poverty and inequality in developing countries.

♣ **Centre for Nonprofit Management (CNM)** (www.cnm.tcd.ie)
School of Business, Trinity College, Dublin 2. T: (01) 896 3850 /
E: **nonprofit@tcd.ie**
CNM supports and develops research, education and dialogue about the Third Sector and non-profit organisations by creating and facilitating relationships across disciplines and sectors. The website includes a resources section with recommended readings, articles and papers. The Centre also hosts speakers on occasion.

♣ **Centre for the Study of Wider Europe (CSWE)** (www.widereurope.ie)
National University of Ireland, Maynooth, Co. Kildare. E: cswe@nuim.ie
A dedicated inter-disciplinary research and teaching centre on Central, Eastern and Southeastern Europe based in NUI Maynooth. Aside from promoting scholarship on this region, CSWE seeks to develop academic and professional links between Ireland and Central, Eastern and Southeastern Europe. The Centre hosts public seminars, which seek to promote understanding of the region's diverse historical, social, cultural and political features. CSWE's website has a selection of web-based resources on Central, Eastern and Southeastern Europe.

Child Info (www.childinfo.org)
This UNICEF website contains statistical data on child-related topics across the globe, including Central and Eastern Europe. Users can access country profiles, regional statistics and reports on topics, such as child health and education. The site also produces an eNewsletter.

Children's Rights Information Network (CRIN) (www.crin.org)
CRIN monitors children's rights across the world and analyses the actions and responses of international bodies. The website informs users on national and international children's rights laws, contains over 21,000 related resources and has a useful A-to-Z of child rights, which translates the jargon associated with child rights into plain English. Users can get help with various related

matters, such as media activities, strategic litigation cases or how to submit reports to the Committee on the Rights of the Child. The CRIN website also contains several useful and informative publications, amongst them:
- *Family Matters: a Study of Institutional Childcare in Central and Eastern Europe and the Former Soviet Union*, 2005.

CIA World Factbook (www.cia.gov/library/publications/the-world-factbook)
A comprehensive source of information on countries and regions, the World Factbook provides an overview of the history, people, government, economy, geography, communications, and infrastructure for over 250 countries and territories across the world.

♣ **Comhlámh** (www.comhlamh.org)
2nd Floor, Ballast House, Aston Quay, Dublin 2. T: (01) 478 3490 / E: info@comhlamh.org
Comhlámh, the Irish Association of Development Workers, is a member and supporter organisation open to anyone interested in social justice, human rights and global development issues. One of Comhlámh's key functions is the provision of support services to those interested in or those who have returned from volunteering or working in development overseas. These services include one-to-one advice, pre-departure training and post-return counseling, debriefing and careers advice. Comhlámh have developed:
- *Volunteer Charter & Code of Good Practice for Sending Organisations.*

Comhlámh also operates **Volunteering Options** (www.volunteeringoptions.org), which provides information for volunteers going overseas and hosts a directory of overseas placements. Comhlámh publications, which are available to download or buy on the website, include:
- *Working for a Better World: A Guide to Volunteering in Global Development*, 2007.
- *The Coming Home Book*, 2010.

♣ **CommunityNI** (www.communityni.org)
CommunityNI is a site for the voluntary and community sector in Northern Ireland, which allows those involved in the sector to network and share news and information on events, jobs and training. The site contains a directory listing more than 5,000 voluntary and community organisations throughout

Northern Ireland. It also hosts an issue-focused forum, which allows individuals involved in the non-profit sector to connect and share their expertise with their peers.

The Community Toolbox (ctb.ku.edu)
This resource is a project of the Work Group for Community Health and Development at the University of Kansas. The project aims to promote community health and development by connecting people, ideas and resources, and provides detailed information and tools to support community development projects.

Consultative Group to Assist the Poor (CGAP) (www.cgap.org)
This website is one of the leading online sources of information on microfinance. Besides a wealth of information on microfinance, the webpage displays training materials from courses and links to other useful microfinance web pages. CGAP also manages **Microfinance Gateway** (www.microfinancegateway.org), which contains thousands of documents, training resources and links.

♣ Department of Community, Equality and Gaeltacht Affairs (www.pobail.ie)
43-49 Mespil Road, Dublin 4. T: (01) 647 3247/ 3017
The website for the Department of Community, Equality and Gaeltacht Affairs details information on the legal framework governing the operation of charities in the Republic of Ireland in the section Charities Regulation, including: Text of the Charities Act 2009; FAQ on the Act; Principle Features of the Charities Act 2009.

♣ Department of Foreign Affairs (www.dfa.ie)
80 St. Stephen's Green, Dublin 2. T: (01) 478 0822 / LoCall: 1890 426 700
The Foreign Affairs website contains travel information on topics such as passports, visas and insurance, as well as specific country updates and risks. It also includes the contact details of Irish embassies and consulates abroad and information on foreign embassies and consulates in Ireland.

♣ **DevelopmentEducation.ie** (www.developmenteducation.ie)
c/o 80:20 Educating and Acting for a Better World, St. Cronans BNS, Vevay Road, Bray, Co. Wicklow. T: (01) 286 0487 /
E: contact@developmenteducation.ie
This website contains a wide range of development and human rights education resources. The website contains downloadable modules, a cartoon gallery, photo stories, a glossary of keywords and definitions, reviews of key resources, opinion pieces from around the world, animations, development 'Top 10s', stimulus sheets, world book reviews, and a host of other innovative teaching supports.

DevelopmentProfessionals.org (www.developmentprofessionals.org)
This is a social networking website, focusing on NGOs and non-profit professionals, civil society groups, development practitioners, community leaders, donors, and academics. Members can post their profile on the website, learn about others working on similar issues, network with colleagues in other parts of the world, establish collective groups with like-minded individuals and seek and respond to questions in forums. There is also an extensive jobs section.

Directory of Development Organisations (www.devdir.org)
Online guide listing over 60,000 development organisations around the world. The directory can be used to search for up-to-date information on not-for-profit organisations and groups working in a particular country.
It is a comprehensive reference tool for identifying service providers, possible project partners or institutions, agencies and programmes. It also includes information on funders and has a jobs notice board. The directory has a section specifically dedicated to Europe, including the countries of Central and Eastern Europe.

♣ **Dóchas** (www.dochas.ie)
12 Harcourt Street, Dublin 2. T: (01) 405 3801
Dóchas is the umbrella organisation of Irish Non-Governmental Organisations (NGOs) involved in development and relief overseas and/or development education in Ireland. Dóchas aims to provide a forum for consultation and cooperation among its members as well as to help them

speak with a single voice on development issues. Dóchas has developed two key codes for overseas charities, which are available on its website:
- *Code of Conduct on Images and Messages*, 2006.
- *Irish Development NGOs Code of Corporate Governance*, 2008.

Dóchas also produces a free weekly eNewsletter, *Wednesday News*, which contains news relevant to the Irish development sector, such as information on meetings, seminars, conferences and workshops; situations vacant (including internship and volunteering opportunities); and notification of forthcoming courses and training opportunities.

♣ Development Training and Learning at Kimmage (Dtalk)
(www.dtalk.ie)
Kimmage Development Studies Centre, Kimmage Manor, Whitehall Road, Dublin 12. T: (01) 406 4341/07 / E: dtalk@kimmagedsc.ie
Dtalk is a training and learning programme, supported by Irish Aid, for development workers from the civil society sector active in international development. This includes Irish NGOs and missionary organisations. The programme is managed by a consortium of organisations led by the Kimmage Development Studies Centre (KDSC – Dublin). Currently, Dtalk is running more than twenty open training courses focusing on management for development results (MfDR) and Communications and Finance. Dtalk can also provide tailor made trainings on any of the topics covered in the ongoing open training courses.

♣ Eastern Europe Aid and Development Network (EEADN)
(www.easterneurope.ie)
EEADN is a network of Irish charities working in Central and Eastern Europe. The site features a news blog, details of network activities, a members directory, and stories of volunteers and development workers who have been or are currently engaged in the region. EEADN also hosts conference and workshop events.

♣ ENCLUDE (www.enclude.ie)
Drumcondra Business Centre, 120 Drumcondra Road, Dublin 9.
T: (01) 653 5099 / E: info@enclude.ie
ENCLUDE is an independent non-profit IT consultancy service for the Irish

non-profit sector, motivated to bridge the 'digital divide', which exists between the commercial and public sectors and the non-profit sector in Ireland. ENCLUDE also offers the ENCLUDEit Programme, which enables eligible Irish non-profit organisations to gain access to a wide range of donated technology products from donor partners, such as Microsoft, Cisco, and Symantec.

EuropeAid (ec.europa.eu/europeaid)
EuropeAid is the EU Directorate–General (DG), which designs the development policy of the EU and awards grants and tenders to implement projects that relate to the EU's external aid programmes. The website provides detailed information on how to access funding, funding procedures and beneficiaries. There is also a link to PADOR (Potential Applicant Data Online Registration), the EU's online registration form for grants specifically for applicants from civil society.

♣ **European Anti-Poverty Network (EAPN)** (www.eapn.org) and
EAPN Ireland (www.eapn.ie)
22 Strand House, Great Strand Street, Dublin 1. T: (01) 8745737
E: info@eapn.ie
An independent network of NGOs and groups involved in the fight to eradicate poverty and social exclusion in the member states of the EU. The EAPN website is a reference portal on poverty and social exclusion in Europe. EAPN have produced a range of publications on topics such as poverty, social inclusion, employment, social protection, EU Structural Funds and the future of Europe, which are available to download on the website.

European Coalition for Community Living (ECCL)
(www.community-living.info)
A Europe-wide initiative which promotes the social inclusion of people with disabilities through the advocacy of community-based services as an alternative to institutionalisation. ECCL's website allows users to access the organisation's eNewsletter and other publications, such as:
- *Focus on the Rights of Children with Disabilities to Live in the Community*, 2006.
- *Included in Society: Results and Recommendations of the European*

Research Initiative on Community-Based Residential Alternatives for Disabled People, 2003.
- *Creating Successful Campaigns for Community Living, An Advocacy Manual for Disability Organisations and Service Providers*, 2006.

♣ European Commission in Ireland (ec.europa.eu/ireland)
European Union House, 18 Dawson Street, Dublin 2. T: (01) 634 1111
The European Commission Representation in Ireland provides information on European affairs to the Irish media and general public. The public can obtain information on the European Commission and the EU from the Representation's website and from the Dawson Street Public Information Centre. The website also provides details of the network of EU information providers in local libraries, business information centres and universities throughout the country and information on the funding available to NGOs, civil society groups and individuals under the different policy areas of the Commission.

European Volunteer Centre – Centre Européen du Volontariat
(www.cev.be)
A European network of over eighty national and regional volunteer centres and development agencies that work to support and promote voluntary activity and to communicate the priorities and concerns of its members to the various institutions of the European Union. CEV's interactive website promotes good practice in volunteering by means of knowledge sharing, structured dialogue and network-building, and is a central forum for the communication and exchange of European policy, practice and information on volunteering. CEV produces a monthly electronic news bulletin, *CEV News* and organises conferences, seminars, workshops and meetings for its members.

FundsForNGOs.org (www.fundsforngos.org)
FundsForNGOs.org is an American initiative which contains up-to-date information about Foundation Funds, Bi-lateral/ Multi-Lateral Fund, for overseas development. It also provides suggestions of alternative methods of funding and developing NGOs long-term. The Resources section includes a number of 'how to' guides and factsheets on a range of topics, such as: How

to write a Proposal, How to develop Logical Framework Analysis (LFA) for Grant Proposals, How to train NGO staff in Fundraising.

♣ Fundraising Ireland (www.fundraisingireland.ie)
3rd Floor, La Touche House, 1 Grove Road, Rathmines, Dublin 6.
T: (01) 407 1613 / E: info@fundraisingireland.ie
Fundraising Ireland offers training and advice to professional fundraisers in Ireland and allows them the opportunity to become part of a large support network. The association hosts an annual conference and regular training seminars, which provide practical advice from domestic and international experts on fundraising-related issues. The website contains a directory of organisations to support and assist fundraisers and also the Fundraising Ireland Code:

- *Code of Professional Conduct for Fundraisers.* Members of Fundraising Ireland are obliged to adhere to the Code, which promotes good practice across the sector.

♣ Institute of International and European Affairs (IIEA)
(www.iiea.com)
8 North Great Georges Street, Dublin 1. T: (01) 8746756 / E: reception@iiea.com
The IIEA is Ireland's leading think tank on European and International affairs. Its research programme aims to provide its members with high-level analysis and forecasts of the challenges on the global and EU policy agendas which impact on Ireland. One of the Institute's theme areas is 'the wider Europe' and it regularly hosts international speakers in Ireland.

♣ Irish Charities Tax Research (ICTR) (www.ictr.ie)
10 Grattan Crescent, Inchicore, Dublin 8. T: (01) 400 2100 / E: ictr@ictr.ie
The ICTR advocates for a policy climate, where regulatory reform and appropriate taxation mean that philanthropy can thrive. Publications, which are available to download from the site, include:

- *The Statement of Guiding Principles for Fundraising,* 2009.
- *Charitable Fundraising in an Economic Downturn,* 2009.

The website provides non-profit organisations with a set of resources to assist them in their efforts to implement the *Guiding Principles,* including:

Compliance Checklist; Public Compliance Statement; Donor Charter; Sample Feedback and Complaints Procedures.

♣ Irish Development Education Association (IDEA)
(www.ideaonline.ie)
5 Merrion Row, Dublin 2. T: (01) 661 8831 / E: info@ideaonline.ie
IDEA works to support the Irish development education sector. The website contains the latest sector-related news and events, a blog, a forum for comment and debate, articles and publications, links to related websites or organisations with shared values, and a network for members. Members can join the IDEA Research Community, which entitles them to attend IDEA workshops and skills-based trainings on research methods and to receive updates from IDEA on development education research.

Inclusion Europe (www.inclusion-europe.org)
Online information service on the European community of persons with intellectual disabilities, which is updated several times per week. Inclusion Europe publications include: *E-include*, Inclusion Europe's online journal (www.e-include.eu).

International Step by Step Association (ISSA) (www.issa.nl)
ISSA promotes equal access to quality education for all children and works with professionals and organisations throughout the world to support programmes that provide education services and advocacy tools to influence policy for families and children. The website contains a database with information on early childhood development and education policy, resources, and initiatives from Central and Eastern Europe.

♣ Irish Aid (www.irishaid.gov.ie)
Riverstone House, 23-27 Henry Street, Limerick. T: (01) 408 2000 / E: irishaid@dfa.ie
Irish Aid is the Irish state's programme of assistance to developing countries. The website gives details of Irish Aid's programmes overseas, as well as information on funding provided and application guidelines.

♣ Irish Aid Volunteering & Information Centre
(www.irishaid.gov.ie/centre)
27-31 Upper O'Connell Street, Dublin 1. LoCall 1890 252 676 /
E: irishaidcentre@dfa.ie
A multi-media exhibition space in Dublin's city centre which is open to the public. Interactive kiosks provide an introduction to overseas volunteering and information on volunteering opportunities. The Centre is also a venue for public events relating to overseas development and volunteering. The website contains an online booking request form or NGOs can contact the Centre directly.

♣ Kimmage Development Studies Centre (KDSC)
(www.kimmagedsc.ie)
Kimmage Manor, Whitehall Road, Dublin 12. T: (01) 406 4386 /
E: info@kimmagedsc.ie
A Dublin-based institute specialising in development training and education. KDSC has been providing nationally accredited programmes in development studies at various levels for more than three decades.

KnowHow NonProfit (www.knowhownonprofit.org)
KnowHow NonProfit is a UK-based comprehensive source of expertise on the non-profit sector. A study zone offers users a range of eLearning support tools – from video tutorials to accredited courses. The site's discussion forum provides a platform for those users to exchange information and experience. KnowHow NonProfit also contains introductory guides on all aspects of setting up, managing and working for a non profit organisation, for example: Working for a Non-profit: Your Options; Recruiting & Managing Volunteers; Media Coverage (Press Release Tips, Giving Radio Interviews).

♣ MyCharity.ie (www.mycharity.ie)
Office 512, 8 Dawson Street, Dublin 2. Lo-call: 1890 929 944
A fee based service, offering charities an online presence and the ability to accept donations direct from the public online. Individuals can also create their own unique fundraising page for any event.

♣ NGO-EU Connect (www.ngoeuconnect.ie)

This website is sponsored by the European Commission in Ireland and endeavours to inform Irish NGOs on how they can use the EU and its various institutions to effect change. The site explains how the EU works and gives advice on how NGOs can lobby the EU. It explains what sources of funding are available to Irish NGOs and how to apply for this funding.

NGO Manager (www.ngomanager.org)

NGO Manager is a Swiss initiative aiming to provide information on NGO management. The eLibrary contains over 300 articles and resources, relating to general NGO management, organisational development, performance management, financial management, human resource management, and communications and marketing.

♣ Northern Ireland Council for Voluntary Action (NICVA)
(www.nicva.org)
61 Duncairn Gardens, Belfast, BT15 2GB. T: +44(0)28 9087 7777 /
E: info@nicva.org

NICVA is a membership and representative umbrella body for the entire voluntary and community sector of Northern Ireland. NICVA offers a range of services including governance and charity advice, research, policy and lobbying, training and consultancy. NICVA also operates **Grant Tracker** (www.granttracker.org), which hosts an extensive online library of articles, publications and resources on fundraising-related topics. For an additional fee, users can subscribe to the site, which allows them full access to the database of funders and a range of dedicated grant search tools.

Office of the High Commissioner for Human Rights (www.ohchr.org)

Comprehensive information on human rights issues across the world, including the Convention on the Rights of the Child, Convention on the Rights of Persons with Disability, and the Millennium Development Goals. Substantial resources section and country-specific information.

Open Society Mental Health Initiative (www.osmhi.org)

The Open Society Mental Health Initiative, based in Hungary, promotes the development of community-based alternatives to institutionalisation for people with mental health problems and disabilities in Central and Eastern Europe and the former Soviet Union. The website provides information on disability and human rights issues and contains an extensive resources section, with best practice information, publications and reports, and useful links.

Organisation for Economic Co-operation and Development (OECD) (www.oecd.org)
The OECD promotes policies aimed at improving the economic and social wellbeing of people around the world. The OECD website has an extensive selection of information and statistical data on topics, such as aid and aid effectiveness, poverty, economic development and entrepreneurship. OECD publications available on the website include:
- *Local Innovations for Growth in Central and Eastern Europe*, 2007.
- *Young people in Eastern Europe and Central Asia: from people to action*, 2007.

Overseas Development Institute (www.odi.org.uk)
ODI is Britain's leading independent think tank on international development and humanitarian issues around the world. The comprehensive resources section on the website includes toolkits, position papers and case studies.

Participatory Community Development (participation.110mb.com)
Website created by the International Federation of the Red Cross and Red Crescent, which has useful links and manuals on participative community development techniques in Central and Eastern Europe.

People in Aid (www.peopleinaid.org)
People in Aid helps humanitarian and development organisations to enhance their organisational effectiveness by improving their people management skills. Their website contains an interactive forum and several useful documents, including:
- *The People in Aid Code of Good Practice*, which promotes best practice in the management and support of aid personnel.

Travellers Point (www.travellerspoint.com)
Travellers Point is a useful online travel guide, which includes information

on travelling to the countries of Central and Eastern Europe, including information on the main cities and regions of the individual countries. It also has a bulletin board service, where users can post their travel related queries.

♣ UCD Development Studies Library
(www.ucd.ie – search term > Development Studies Library)
Level 3, James Joyce Library Building, University College Dublin, Belfield, Dublin 4. T: (01) 716 7560 / E: library@ucd.ie
Home to the largest collection of development-related research materials in Ireland, UCD's Development Studies Library is open to members of the public, as well as UCD staff and students.

UNICEF (www.unicef.org)
The United Nations Children's Fund works for the survival, development and protection of children's rights, guided by the Convention on the Rights of the Child. The website contains extensive information on various issues affecting children worldwide, such as child survival and development, basic education and HIV/ AIDS. There is also a section specifically dedicated to Central and Eastern Europe and the CIS, including specific reports and research on the region such as:
- *Children and Disability in Transition in CEE/CIS and Baltic States*, 2005.
- *Changing Minds, Policies and Lives: Improving Protection of Children in Eastern Europe and Central Asia*, 2003.
- *Blame and Banishment: The Underground HIV Epidemic Affecting Children in Eastern Europe and Central Asia*, 2010.

United Nations Volunteers Online (www.onlinevolunteering.org)
A free online volunteer service, which connects volunteers with development organisations around the world. Volunteers contribute their skills and collaborate with organisations online in areas such as web development, graphic design, translation, editing and research.

United Nations Development Programme (www.undp.org)
Information on the United Nations programme of assistance in developing countries, including a section on Central and Eastern Europe and the progress of the Millennium Development Goals. The website also contains

the contact details of UNDP offices in countries across the world.

♣ **Volunteer Centres Ireland** (www.volunteer.ie)
DMG Business Centre, 9-13 Blackhall Place, Dublin 7. T: (01) 7994519 / E: info@volunteer.ie
Volunteer Centres Ireland coordinate a network of volunteer centres around Ireland. They provide a service to match volunteers with charities. The website contains guidelines on recruiting and managing volunteers including: Steps for Setting up a Volunteer Programme, How to Develop a Volunteer Role Description; Garda Vetting, Reference Checks, Volunteer Expenses, Motivating and Thanking Volunteers.

♣ **Volunteering Ireland** (www.volunteeringireland.ie)
Coleraine House, Coleraine Street, Dublin 7. T: (01) 872 2622 / E: info@volunteeringireland.com
Volunteering Ireland works to promote and support high quality voluntary activity in Ireland and overseas. Resources are available on the website including information on: Safeguard Programme (Garda Vetting for Overseas Volunteers), Charter for Effective Volunteering, Volunteer Policies, Supervising Volunteers. The website also contains details of both short- and long-term voluntary positions.

♣ **The Wheel** (www.wheel.ie)
Irish Social Finance Centre, 10 Grattan Crescent, Inchicore, Dublin 8. T: (01) 454 8727 / E: info@wheel.ie
An umbrella network for Irish not-for-profit organisations, operating with a national remit for the Republic of Ireland. The Wheel advocates the effective use of resources and best practice in all non-profit organisations, promotes a better understanding of the sector amongst the public and represents the interests of the sector before Government and other decision-making bodies. Their website operates a forum for and about the non-profit sector in Ireland called **Sector Connector**, where users can post and reply to questions. The Wheel organises regular trainings, conferences and workshops for the sector, covering a range of topics, such as governance, charity regulation, risk management, human resource management and information technology. The Wheel also operates **Funding Point** (www.fundingpoint.ie), a paid

subscription service which allows the user to access information on funding opportunities from Irish and international sources.

The World Bank (www.worldbank.org)

The World Bank's online issue briefs provide an overview of World Bank activities on specific topics in development, such as agriculture and rural development, poverty, children and youth, education, health, disabilities, employment, gender, social development, urban development, microfinance, regional overviews. The World Bank website contains hundreds of publications on development issues, many related to Central and Eastern Europe, including:
- *Moving from Residential Institutions to Community-Based Social Services in Central and Eastern Europe and the Former Soviet Union*, World Bank, 2000.
- *Supporting a healthy transition: lessons from early World Bank experience in Eastern Europe*, 2002.

World Health Organisation (WHO) (www.who.int)

WHO is the UN agency responsible for providing leadership on global health matters, shaping the health research agenda, setting norms and standards, developing policy, providing technical support to countries and monitoring and assessing health trends. The website for the **WHO Regional Office for Europe** (www.euro.who.int) gives information on their work in European countries, including the countries of Central and Eastern Europe. This key resource provides authoritative health data on the 53 countries in the WHO European Region.